CREATIVE CLOTHES
AND ACCESSORIES
FOR CHILDREN

First published in 1998 by
Sally Milner Publishing Pty Ltd
RMB 54 Burra Road
Burra Creek NSW 2620
Australia

© Kathleen Blaxland, 1998

Edited by Felicity Hunt
Designed by Anna Warren, Warren Ventures, Sydney
Printed and bound in China

National Library of Australia Cataloguing-in-Publication data:

Blaxland, Kathleen.
  Creative clothing & accessories for children.

  Includes index.
  ISBN 1 86351 213 6

  1. Children's clothing. 2. Dressmaking. 3. Sewing.
  I. Title. (Series: Milner craft series).

646.406

CREATIVE CLOTHES AND ACCESSORIES FOR CHILDREN

SALLY MILNER PUBLISHING

To my Grandchildren, the models, Ashlee, Kaitlin, Mathew and Laura, with love.

Special thanks to Barry Nancarrow of Barry Nancarrow Productions, still photographic and video production services, 11 Hudson Street, Hamilton, NSW, Australia

Contents

Introduction

How often have you looked at magazines with pictures of children in beautiful 'olde worlde' garments and wished you could create such beautiful fashions? This book will help you achieve that wish.

You will find yourself returning to an era when home sewing was easy and rewarding and had the added benefit of saving costs.

Just follow these easy-to-draft patterns and step-by-step sewing instructions to complete the garments with a professional finish.

Included are patterns for pretty flower girl frocks, handsome page boy suits and cute party frocks. The accessories include handmade roses, detachable collars with a hint of beading for a look of glamour and many more.

There is also a special section on sewing fancy dress costumes for the theatre and parties, or simply dressing up for a fun photo shoot that captures happy childhood memories.

Before you begin any pattern in this book refer to the section *Before You Start to Sew* on page 8 for tips on how to adjust pattern sizes and how to cut the fabric. Individual chapters outline in detail how to complete each garment and include both metric and imperial measurements.

The section on *Sewing Techniques* provides further detailed instructions on the most commonly used techniques such as setting in sleeves and zips, making bindings, rouleaus and button loops, and fluting edges.

Before You Start to Sew

By carefully following the diagrams and instructions in this book a complete copy of the garments illustrated can be achieved.

SIZES

The patterns are drawn to the scale 1:4 ie. 1cm = 4cm (1in = 4in). The quantity of material and the size of each pattern can be adjusted according to a child's individual fitting.

CUTTING THE PATTERN

The same rules apply to cutting out from your pattern as the guide sheet of a commercial pattern.

- Always press the paper pattern and your material with a warm iron to remove any creases.
- Always pin the pattern to the wrong side of the material.
- Follow lengthwise and cross grain arrows to keep the material on the correct grain line.

PREPARING TO CUT THE FABRIC

- Use a pin to mark the right side of the material as this saves time when assembling the garment.
- Start placing the pins from the top of the pattern pieces and work downwards, pressing any creases down towards the bottom as you continue pinning.
- Transfer all pattern markings onto the material before removing the pattern.
- Keep one hand on the pattern pieces while cutting out and keep the material lying flat.

TOILE

Cut out a calico toile (practice copy) of the garment you intend to make and perfect the pattern before cutting out your fabric. Darts and seam lines can be marked on the toile with biro to help give a correct fitting.

Creative Clothes

1. SILK TARTAN FROCK

Pattern designed to fit 5 year old

MATERIALS

    1.8m (2yd) of 44cm (17 ½in) wide silk tartan

    1m (1⅛yd) of 90cm (36in) wide black velvet (for top)

    1.8m (2yd) of 90cm (36in) wide black taffeta (for petticoat)

    45cm (½yd) of 90cm (36in) wide black satin (for bindings)

    1 reel black polyester thread

    30.5cm (12in) black zip

METHOD

1.   Machine shoulder seams of bodice. Repeat with lining. (Fig 1.1)

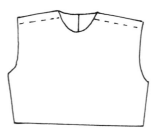

Fig 1.1 Machine shoulder seams of bodice. Repeat with lining.

2.   To make ruffles around edge of collar, measure neck edge of the two collars and cut two strips the same length by 5cm (2in) wide. Fold in half length-wise, wrong sides facing together, and press flat. Machine a 14mm (½in) gathering stitch along the edge of each strip. (Fig 1.2) Pull up gathering stitch and pin ruffles to collars, evenly distributing gathers. Tack in place.

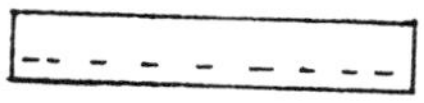

Fig 1.2 Machine a gathering stitch on seam line of ruffles.

3. To make a binding for edge of collar, cut a 4cm (1½in) wide bias binding from the black satin material the same length as collar edge. *Refer to Bindings on page 106.*

4. Pin bindings on top of ruffles, then tack and machine together using a zipper foot. (Fig 1.3)

Fig 1.3 Machine ruffles and satin bindings to collars.

5. Pin and tack the two backs of collar sections, right sides facing together, and machine along seam line. (Fig 1.4) Trim edges and clip curves. Turn to right side and press. Change zipper foot back to basic foot.

Fig 1.4 Machine the two backs to the collars.

6. On right side of bodice, pin the two collars to neck edge, tack and machine. Pin right side of bodice to lining facing. Pin, tack and machine around neck area and down each side of back bodice. Trim any bulk from seams and turn to right side. Press flat. (Fig 1.5)

7. Machine side seams of bodice and lining and press flat. (Fig 1.5)

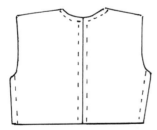

Fig 1.5 Machine around neck area and down each side of back bodice. Machine side seams of bodice and lining.

8. Measure waist area of bodice and cut a binding from the black satin material. Machine binding to waistline using a zipper foot. *Refer to Bindings on page 106.* (Fig 1.6)

Fig 1.6 Machine binding on waistline.

9. Machine front and back skirt sections together, leaving an opening above circle for zip. Repeat with petticoat. Machine gathering stitch along upper edge of both skirt and petticoat. With wrong sides facing, gather skirt and petticoat to fit waist area. Pin, tack and machine skirt and petticoat together. (Fig 1.7)

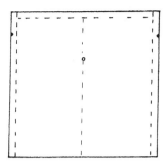

Fig 1.7 Machine seams of skirt and petticoat. Gather up waistlines.

10. On right side of bodice and above piping, pin bodice to skirt matching side and centre back seams. Change to a zipper foot and sew close to piping edge. Tack and machine together. (Fig 1.8)

Fig 1.8 Machine bodice to skirt. Machine in the zip. Machine hemlines.

11. Machine zip in back. *Refer to Setting in a Zip on page 96.*

12. Press up a 7.5cm (3in) hem on skirt and machine. Repeat with petticoat.

13. Gather up bottom edges of sleeves to fit width of arms. To make sleeve ruffles, cut two strips the length of the sleeves and 5cm (2in) wide (using the method described in Step 2 for collar ruffles). Pin, tack and machine ruffles to bottom of sleeves. Make a satin binding (using the same method as described in Steps 2 and 3 for collar bindings) and tack on seams of ruffles using a zipper foot. (Fig 1.9)

Fig 1.9 Machine ruffles and bindings to sleeves.

14. With right sides facing each other, pin, tack and machine cuffs to sleeves. (Fig 1.10)

15. Machine seams of sleeves and cuffs. (Fig 1.11) Turn sleeves to right side and, on the inside, fold over seam of cuff and hand-stitch along the edge.

Fig 1.10 Machine cuffs to sleeves.

Fig 1.11 Machine seams of sleeves.

16. Machine sleeves into armholes. (Fig 1.12) *Refer to Sleeves on page 102.*

Fig 1.12 Machine sleeves into armholes.

17. To make bows, fold each strip in half length-wise with right sides facing together. Machine on seam line and leave an opening at each end.

18. Fasten a safety pin at one end and pull through to right side. Press flat.

    Fold each end of one strip to the centre and hand-stitch with a needle and thread.

20. Cut three strips, 4cm (1½in) long and 5cm (2in) wide, to make centres of bows. Press a 14mm (½in) fold over each side. Bind around centre of bow and catch with a needle and thread at back of bow. Repeat with other two bows.

21. Measure from centre of neckline to waistline and mark evenly the position of the three bows. Hand-stitch bows to bodice. (Fig 1.13)

Fig 1.13 Machine three bows for bodice. Measure from centre of neck to waistline and evenly hand-stitch bows to bodice.

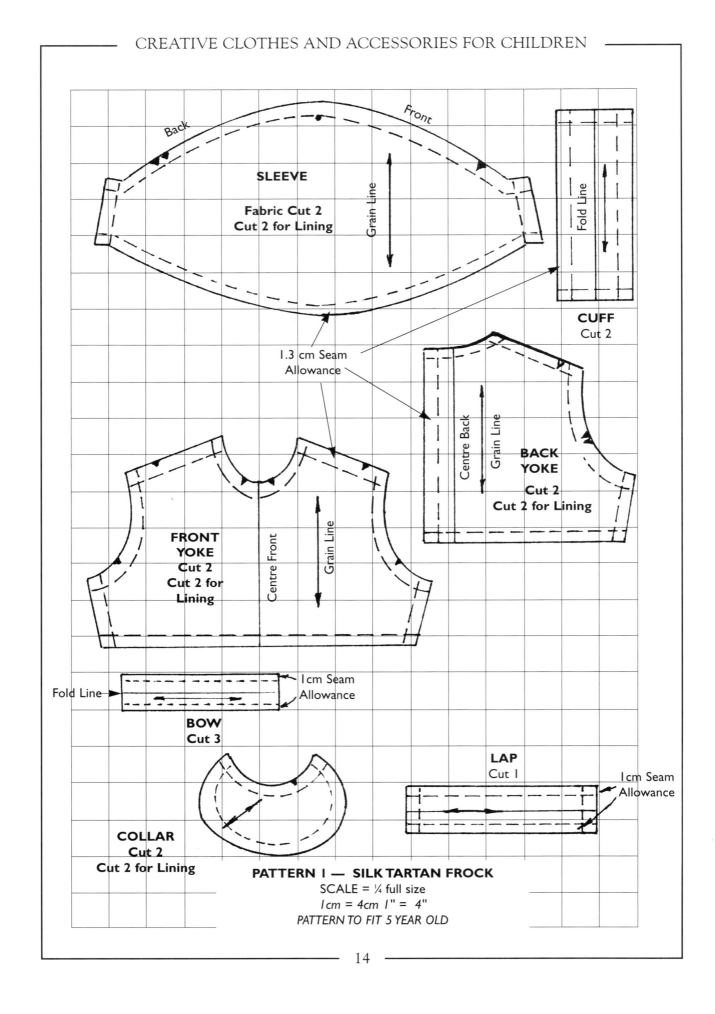

SLEEVE

Fabric Cut 2
Cut 2 for Lining

Back

Front

Grain Line

Fold Line

CUFF
Cut 2

1.3 cm Seam
Allowance

BACK
YOKE

Cut 2
Cut 2 for Lining

Centre Back

Grain Line

FRONT
YOKE
Cut 2
Cut 2 for
Lining

Centre Front

Grain Line

Fold Line

1cm Seam
Allowance

BOW
Cut 3

COLLAR
Cut 2

Cut 2 for Lining

LAP
Cut 1

1cm Seam
Allowance

PATTERN 1 — SILK TARTAN FROCK
SCALE = ¼ full size
1cm = 4cm 1" = 4"
PATTERN TO FIT 5 YEAR OLD

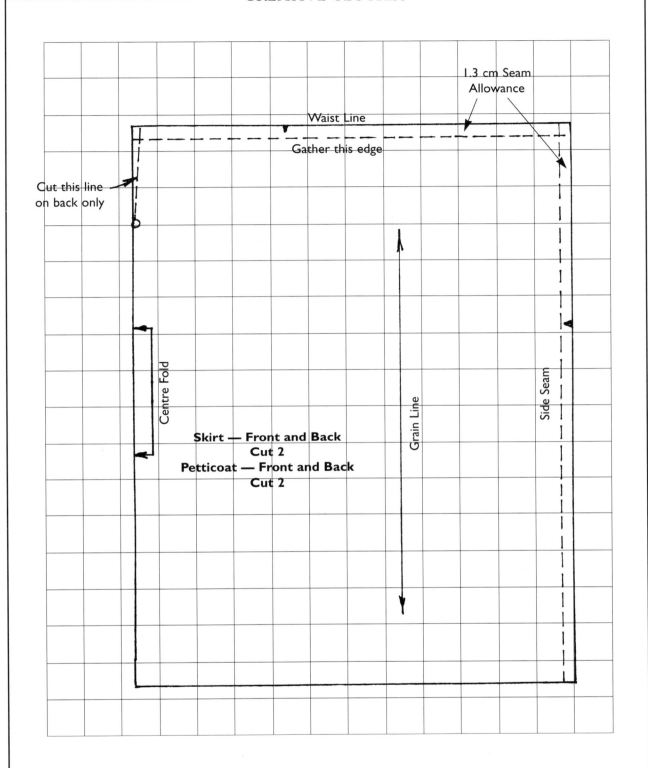

1.3 cm Seam Allowance

Waist Line

Gather this edge

Cut this line on back only

Centre Fold

Grain Line

Side Seam

Skirt — Front and Back
Cut 2
Petticoat — Front and Back
Cut 2

PATTERN 1 — SILK TARTAN FROCK (cont)
SCALE = ¼ full size
1cm = 4cm 1" = 4"
PATTERN TO FIT 5 YEAR OLD

2. VELVET AND SILK FROCK

This frock with its velvet bodice, delicate lace neck ruffle and long lace-trimmed sleeves has a look of beautiful Parisian elegance.

Pattern designed to fit 5 year old

MATERIALS

    1.8m (2yd) of 115cm (45in) wide black velvet (for bodice and sleeves)

    1.8m (2yd) of 115cm (45in) wide silk taffeta (for skirt and sash)

    1.8m (2yd) of 90cm (36in) wide matching taffeta (for petticoat)

    1.8m (2yd) of 10cm (4in) wide fine white lace (for neck and sleeve frill)

    35cm (14in) zip.

    2 reels matching polyester thread

METHOD

Bodice

1. Machine shoulder seams of bodice. Repeat with lining. (Fig 2.1)

Fig 2.1 Machine shoulder seams of bodice. Repeat with lining.

Fig 2.2 Machine lace frill to neckline.

2. Cut a 55cm (22in) length of lace for neck frill. Machine a 14mm (½in) seam at each end. Machine a gathering stitch along straight edge.

3. Pull up gathering thread evenly to fit neckline. With right sides of bodice and lace frill facing together, pin, tack and machine lace frill to neckline. (Fig 2.2)

4. With right sides of bodice and lining facing together, pin and tack around neckline and down back zip opening. (Fig 2.3) Cut away any bulk on seams and neckline.

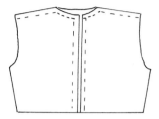

Fig 2.3 With right sides of bodice and lining facing together, machine around neckline and down back zip opening.

5. Turn lining to inside of bodice and press flat. Machine around neckline and down back zip opening. Machine raw edges and press seams flat, ready to set in the zip.

Back Sashes

1. With right sides facing together, machine on seam lines of ties. Pull to right side through end openings. Press flat. (Fig 2.4A)
2. Fold in 14mm (½in) at raw edges of ties and machine a row of gathering. Pull up thread to half the width of ties. (Fig 2.4B)

Fig 2.4A Machine ties on seam line.

Fig 2.4B Pull up gathering at open end of ties.

Fig 2.5 Machine sides of skirt and back seam up to the circle. Repeat with lining.

Skirt and petticoat

1. Machine front and back skirt sections together at side seams. (Fig 2.5) Overlock seams and press flat.
2. Machine centre back seam in skirt leaving opening above circle for zip. Repeat with lining. (Fig 2.5)
3. Machine a gathering stitch on upper edge of skirt and petticoat.

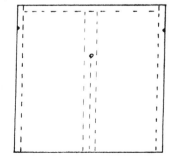

4. With wrong sides facing each other, gather skirt and petticoat to fit waist area. Pin, tack and machine skirt and petticoat together. With right sides facing together, pin skirt to bodice matching centre, side and back seams. (Fig 2.6)

5. Set in zip. (Fig 2.6) *Refer to Setting in a Zip on page 100.*

Fig 2.6 Machine skirt to bodice. Set in zip.

6. Press and fold up a 5cm (2in) hem on skirt. Repeat with petticoat. Machine close to edges of hems.

Sleeves

1. Machine seams of sleeves and sleeve linings. (Fig 2.7) Press seams flat open.

2. Cut two 25cm (10in) lengths of lace for cuffs. Join a 14mm (½in) seam at each end and neaten. Press seams flat.

3. Gather up lace along straight edge to fit end of sleeve.

4. With seams matching and right sides of velvet and lace frill facing each other, pin, tack and machine lace to end of sleeve. (Fig 2.8) Neaten edges and press seam towards top of sleeve. Repeat steps 2 and 3 for second sleeve.

Fig 2.7 Machine seams of sleeves and sleeve linings.

Fig 2.8 Machine lace cuffs to sleeves.

5. Turn sleeve to right side and drop lining into sleeve. Match side seams and front and back notches at top of sleeve. Baste sleeve and sleeve lining together. Repeat for second sleeve.

6. Set sleeves into armholes. (Fig 2.9) *Refer to Sleeves on page 102.*

7. At bottom edges of sleeves and sleeve linings, fold up 14mm (½in) and press. Pin and hand-stitch lining to lace frill.

8. Pin and tack sashes at each side seam with right side of material facing back bodice. Machine. (Fig 2.9)

9. Machine hems of dress and petticoat.

Fig 2.9 Machine sleeves into armholes. Machine hems of frock and petticoat. Machine ties to side seams of back bodice.

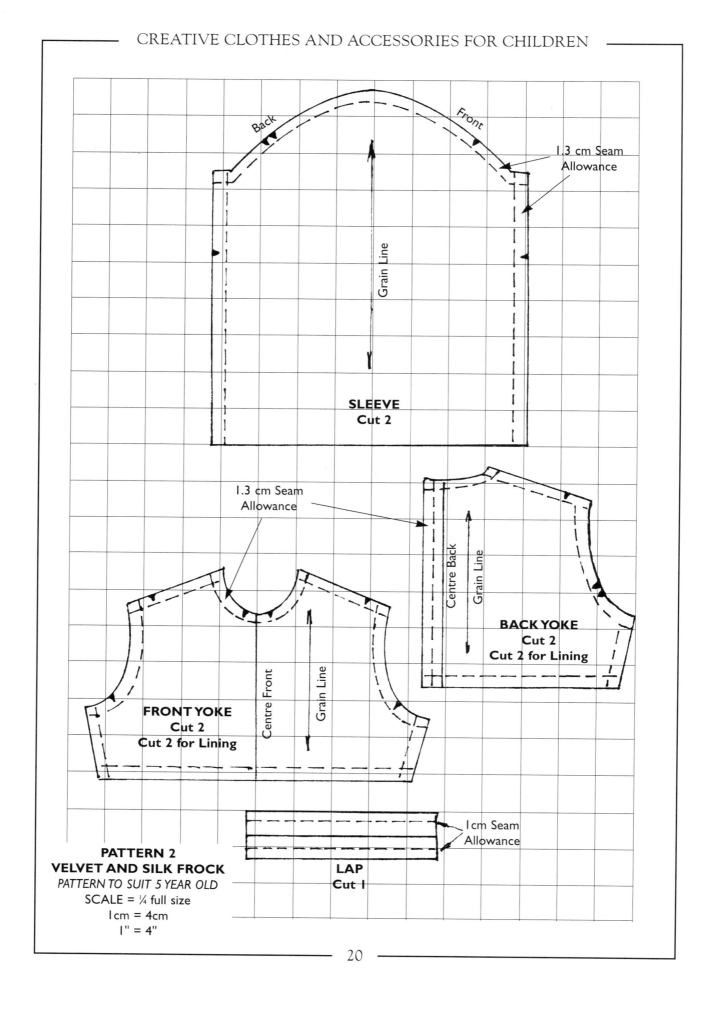

SLEEVE
Cut 2

1.3 cm Seam Allowance

Grain Line

Back

Front

1.3 cm Seam Allowance

Centre Back

Grain Line

BACK YOKE
Cut 2
Cut 2 for Lining

FRONT YOKE
Cut 2
Cut 2 for Lining

Centre Front

Grain Line

LAP
Cut 1

1cm Seam Allowance

PATTERN 2
VELVET AND SILK FROCK
PATTERN TO SUIT 5 YEAR OLD
SCALE = ¼ full size
1cm = 4cm
1" = 4"

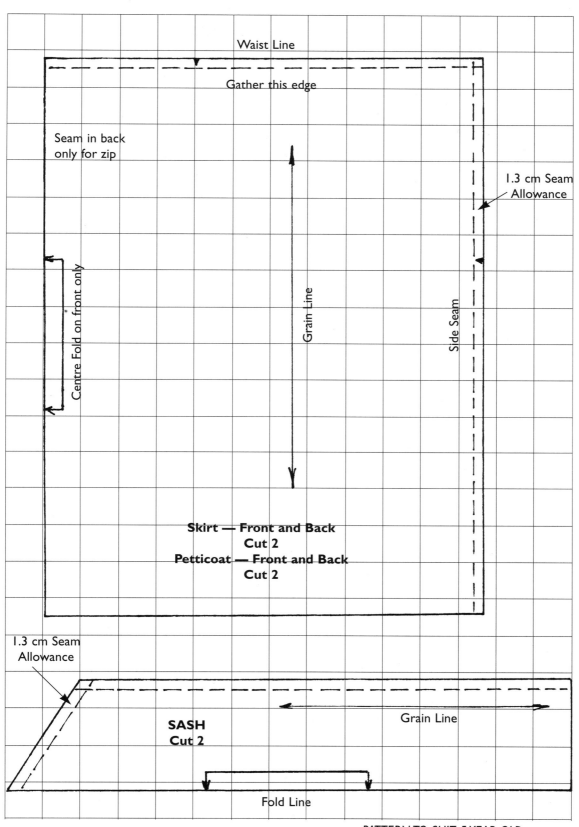

Waist Line

Gather this edge

Seam in back
only for zip

1.3 cm Seam
Allowance

Centre Fold on front only

Grain Line

Side Seam

**Skirt — Front and Back
Cut 2
Petticoat — Front and Back
Cut 2**

1.3 cm Seam
Allowance

**SASH
Cut 2**

Grain Line

Fold Line

**PATTERN 2
VELVET AND SILK FROCK
(cont)**

PATTERN TO SUIT 5 YEAR OLD
SCALE = ¼ full size
1cm = 4cm
1" = 4"

3. PINK BROCADE FROCK AND MATCHING HAT

A beautiful frock with a matching hat always gives an air of elegance. The cream lace bodice and puff sleeves compliment the floral brocade skirt. The attached petticoat is decorated with a lace border and the cream straw hat is trimmed with handmade silk roses.

Pattern designed to fit 5 year old

MATERIALS

2.75m (3yd) of 115cm (45in) wide floral brocade material

1.8m (2yd) of 90cm (36in) wide cream lace

1.8m (2yd) cream polyester material (for petticoat)

1.8m (2yd) of 4cm (1½in) wide cream lace (for edge of petticoat)

1 reel pink polyester thread

1 reel cream polyester thread

1.8m (2yd) of 4cm (1½in) wide cream lace for roses

90cm (1yd) of 2.5cm (1in) wide pink lace for roses

17 covered brocade buttons

METHOD

Bodice

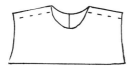

Fig 3.1 Machine shoulder seams of lace bodice.

1. Pin and machine front and back lace yoke sections at shoulders. (Fig 3.1) Repeat with other two lace sections (which become the lining).

2. Machine a small hem along edge of neck frill. Tack and machine lace on the edge of the frill. (Fig 3.2) Gather up frill and machine frill to neck area, right sides together. (Fig 3.3)

Fig 3.2 Machine lace to neck frill.

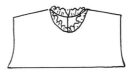

Fig 3.3 Stitch frill to neck edge.

3. Sew a rouleau from the brocade material long enough to make 17 loops for back section to correspond with covered buttons. *Refer to Rouleaus on page 104.*

4. Pin and tack seven loops evenly in place on left-hand side of back yoke down to bottom seam edge. (Fig 3.4)

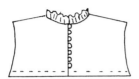

Fig 3.4 Stitch seven loops at back yoke.

5. With right sides of lace bodice and lining facing each other, pin, tack and machine together from the seam edges at the back and all around neck seam. Clip neck edge seam and turn to right side. Press flat. (Fig 3.5)

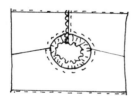

Fig 3.5 Machine yoke and lining together.

6. Machine darts on front and back lower floral sections. Repeat with lining. Cut through centre of darts from the wide end almost to the point. (Fig 3.6) Clip seam allowance to let darts lie flat. Press flat open. With wrong sides facing each other, baste lining and bodice together.

Fig 3.6 Stitch darts.

7. Machine a binding at the top of floral bodice, back and front. *Refer to Bindings on page 106.* (Fig 3.7)

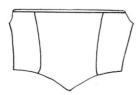

Fig 3.7 Stitch top binding.

8.   Machine a binding each side of shoulder straps. Pin and tack straps to lace bodice where circles indicate on pattern. Machine in place. (Fig 3.8)

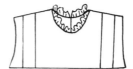

Fig 3.8 Stitch straps to lace bodice.

9.   Pin top and bottom yoke sections (front and back) together on binding. (Fig 3.9)

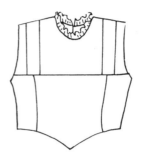

Fig 3.9 Join front lace and floral bodice.

10. Pin, tack and machine 10 more loops down back bodice, following on from top seven loops. Machine side seams of bodice, clip curves and press seams flat.

11. Cut a binding from the brocade material long enough to bind waistline.

Skirt and Petticoat

1.   To reinforce opening in back skirt section, machine on dotted line. Cut along centre back to point. (Fig 3.10)

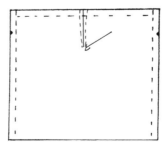

Fig 3.10 Reinforce opening in back skirt.

2. Tack right side of continuous lap to wrong side of back and machine. Press seam allowance towards lap. (Fig 3.11)

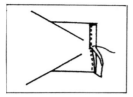

Fig 3.11 Machine continuous lap to back opening.

3. Turn under a 10mm (⅜in) fold on the other edge of lap and stitch over seam on the outside.

4. On the inside bring edges together. Stitch diagonally across lower edge. (Fig 3.12)

Fig 3.12 Machine diagonally across lower edge.

5. Press left edge of lap to inside. Tack to back at upper edge.

6. Machine side seams of skirt. Overlock seams and press towards the back. (Fig 3.13)

7. Machine side seams of petticoat and back seam leaving seam open above notch. Overlock seams and press back seam of petticoat flat open.

8. Machine a gathering stitch along top seam line of skirt and petticoat. (Fig 3.13)

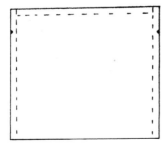

Fig 3.13 Machine side seams, and gathering stitch along top seam line.

9. Pull up gathering stitch in sections to fit waistline of bodice.

10. With wrong sides of skirt and petticoat facing each other, pin, tack and machine together.

11. On right side of bodice and above the piping, pin bodice to skirt matching side and centre back seams. Change to a zipper foot to sew close to piping edge. (Fig 3.14)

Fig 3.14 Machine bodice to skirt.

12. Pin and tack lace on edge of petticoat and machine.
13. Press up a 7.5cm (3in) hem and machine.

Sleeve Armhole Ruffle

1. Press under hem allowance on curved edge of ruffle. Tack and machine lace to right side of curved edge. (Fig 3.15)

Fig 3.15 Machine lace to sleeve ruffle.

2. To gather raw edge of ruffle between large dots, stitch along seam line using a long machine stitch.
3. With right sides facing together, pin ruffle to armhole edge between front and two back notches. Pull up gathering stitch to fit sleeve.
4. Gather up edge of sleeve between notches. Gather lower edge of sleeve.
5. On the outside pin lace to notched edge of cuff. Tack.
6. Press under 1.5cm (⅝in) on unnotched edge of cuff.

7. With right sides facing together, pin cuff to sleeve and distribute gathering to fit. Tack and machine. (Fig 3.16)

8. Stitch seam in sleeve and cuff, and overlock. (Fig 3.17)

Fig 3.16 Machine cuff to sleeve.

Fig 3.17 Stitch seam in sleeve.

9. Turn cuff to inside on fold line. Hand-stitch seam.

10. With right sides together, pin, tack and machine sleeve into armhole matching notches and underarm seams. Overlock edges. (Fig 3.18)

Fig 3.18 Machine sleeves into armholes.

11. Repeat the steps above for second sleeve and cuff. *Refer to Sleeves on page 102.*

Roses

1. Stitch seven lace roses with the pink colour in the centre. (Fig 3.19) *Refer to Cloth Roses on page 96.*

Fig 3.19 Cloth rose.

Fig 3.20 Hand-stitch roses to neck and sleeves. Hand-stitch bows to straps.

2. Hand-stitch three roses in centre of lace neckline and two roses either side in centre of sleeve cuffs. (Fig 3.20)

Bows

1. Fold each strip in half length-wise (right sides together). Machine a 10mm (⅜in) seam allowance leaving an opening at each end.

2. Fasten a safety pin at one end and pull through to right side. Press flat.

3. Fold each end of one strip to the centre and hand-stitch.

4. Cut two squares of material 7.5cm (3in) wide by 7.5cm (3in) long for the centres of the two bows. Press each side of the square 6mm (¼in) over and cut in half. Bind one around the centre of each bow and catch with a needle and thread at the back.

5. Pin bows in the centre of each shoulder strap and stitch at back of bows.

MATCHING HAT

MATERIALS

    Cream coloured straw hat

    70cm (¾yd) of gathered cream lace

    2m (2⅛yd) of 4cm (1½in) wide lace (for crown of hat)

    23cm (¼yd) of pink silk organza material (for roses)

    90cm (1yd) of straight-edged cream lace (for roses)

    1 reel cream thread

    6 small artificial green leaves

    craft glue

METHOD

1. Glue gathered lace around crown of hat.

2. Sew three small cloth roses, three medium-sized roses in pink organza and three lace roses. The number of roses will depend on the size of the hat. *Refer to Cloth Roses on page 96.*

3. Glue roses and leaves evenly to front of hat.

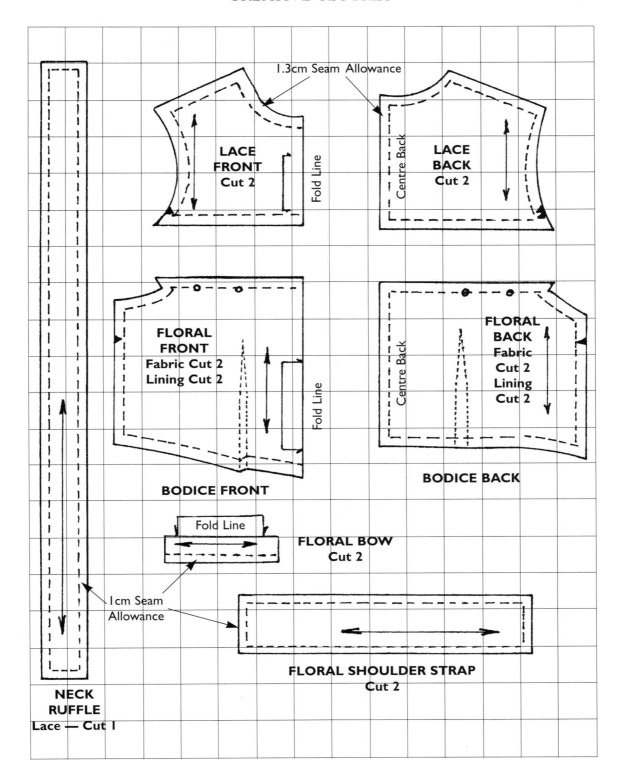

PATTERN 3
PINK BROCADE FROCK
PATTERN TO SUIT 5 YEAR OLD
SCALE = ¼ full size
1cm = 4cm
1" = 4"

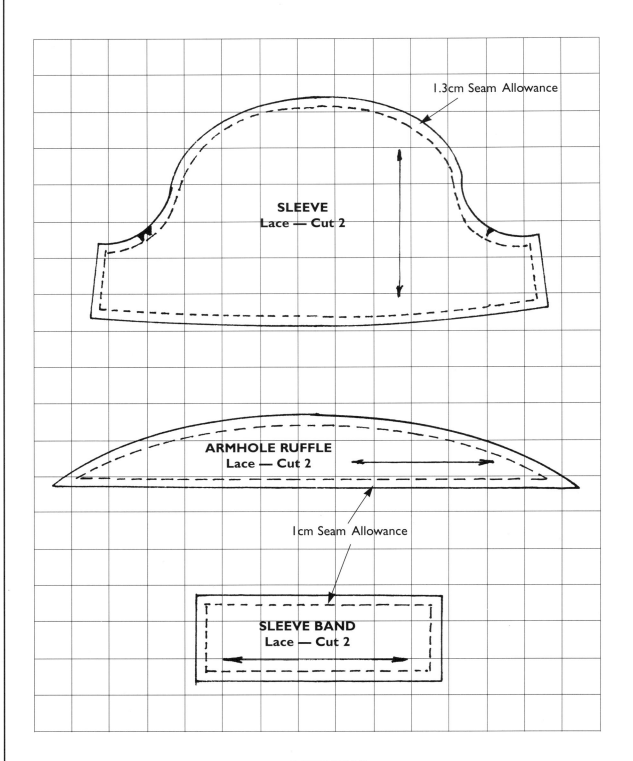

1.3cm Seam Allowance

SLEEVE
Lace — Cut 2

ARMHOLE RUFFLE
Lace — Cut 2

1cm Seam Allowance

SLEEVE BAND
Lace — Cut 2

PATTERN 3
PINK BROCADE FROCK (cont)
PATTERN TO SUIT 5 YEAR OLD
SCALE = ¼ full size
1cm = 4cm
1" = 4"

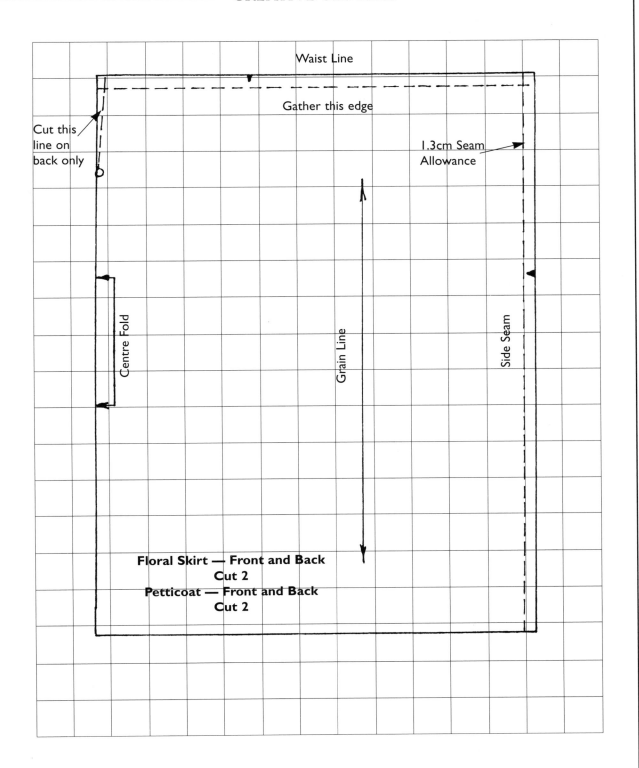

Waist Line

Gather this edge

Cut this line on back only

1.3cm Seam Allowance

Centre Fold

Grain Line

Side Seam

Floral Skirt — Front and Back
Cut 2
Petticoat — Front and Back
Cut 2

PATTERN 3
PINK BROCADE FROCK (cont)
PATTERN TO SUIT 5 YEAR OLD
SCALE = ¼ full size
1cm = 4cm
1" = 4"

4. BLACK VELVET AND WHITE ORGANZA FROCK

This classic frock of black velvet and white organza is a glamorous garment for the autumn and winter seasons. The attached underslip is made of black taffeta with frills and threaded white satin ribbon trimming. Teamed with black lace gloves and top hat the photographic effect is outstanding.

Pattern designed to fit 7 year old

MATERIALS

    3.66m (4yd) of 115cm (45in) wide black velvet

    3.66m (4yd) of 115cm (45in) wide black taffeta

    90cm (1yd) of white organza

    90cm (1yd) of fine white cotton (for lining)

    3.66m (4yd) of 2cm (¾in) wide black silk ribbon (for bodice)

    3.66m (4yd) of 2cm (¾in) wide black eyelet lace (for petticoat ruffle)

    3.66m (4yd) of 6mm (¼in) wide white satin ribbon (for petticoat ruffle)

    35cm (14in) black zip

    2 reels black polyester cotton

    1 reel white polyester cotton

METHOD

Bodice

1. Baste organza centre panel over white lining. (Fig 4.1)

Fig 4.1 Baste organza panel over white lining.

1. Silk Tartan Frock

2. Velvet and Silk Frock

3. PINK BROCADE FROCK AND MATCHING HAT

4. BLACK VELVET AND WHITE ORGANZA FROCK

5. Buccaneer Shirt and Trousers

6. Satin Shortie Pyjamas

7. SILK AND TULLE FLOWER GIRL FROCK

9. Page Boy Suit, 7. Silk and Tulle Flower Girl Frock and
8. Raw Silk Flower Girl Frock

10. FLOWER FAIRY COSTUME

11. Purple and Jade Harem Costumes

12. CLOWN COSTUME

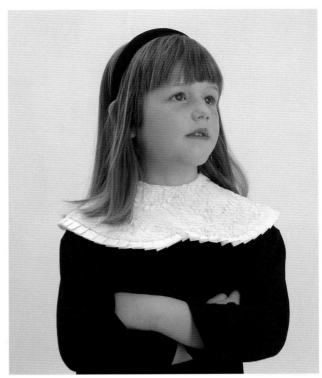

ABOVE LEFT: 13. BLACK VELVET AND LACE COLLAR AND BLACK SNOOD

ABOVE RIGHT: 14. CREAM LACE COLLAR

LEFT: 15. DILLY BAGS WITH BLACK VELVET LACE COLLAR

BELOW: 16. CLOTH ROSES ON HAT

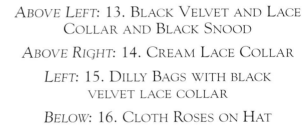

2. Cut and machine an organza binding around neck of panel. *Refer to Bindings on page 106.* (Fig 4.2)

Fig 4.2 Machine a binding around neckline.

3. Place panel pattern on material and mark where the three rows of ribbon are positioned. Pin and tack ribbons in place and machine close to ribbon edges. (Fig 4.3)

Fig 4.3 Machine three rows of ribbon to panel.

4. Hand-stitch 2cm (¾in) pleats with black ribbon, long enough to pin down each side of organza panel. Machine pleated ribbon each side of panel. (Fig 4.4)

Fig 4.4 Machine pleated ribbon each side of panel.

5. With right sides facing together, pin, tack and machine velvet side sections to organza panel. (Fig 4.5) Press flat towards side seams.

6. On wrong side of bodice, baste side lining over velvet side sections. Hand-stitch in place, folding under seam allowance where ribbon has been joined.

Fig 4.5 Machine velvet sides to organza panel.

7. With right sides of back bodice and back lining facing together, machine around neckline and down each side of two back sections. (Fig 4.6)

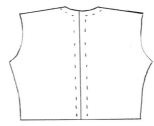

Fig 4.6 With right sides of back bodice and lining facing together, machine around neckline and down each side of two back sections.

8. With right sides facing together, tack and machine bodice front and back at shoulders. Press seams towards the back. Join side seams of back and velvet front together. Repeat with lining so that wrong sides are facing together. (Fig 4.7)

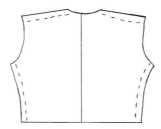

Fig 4.7 With right sides of back bodice and lining facing together, machine shoulder and side seams.

9. Cut and machine a taffeta binding all around waistline. *Refer to Bindings on page 106.* (Fig 4.8)

Fig 4.8 Machine a taffeta binding all around waistline.

Skirt and Petticoat

1. To reinforce opening in back of skirt machine along dotted line. Cut up from bottom to point.

2. Tack right side of continuous lap to wrong side of back opening and machine. (Fig 4.9) Press seam allowance towards lap.

Fig 4.9 Tack right side of continuous lap to wrong side of back.

3. Turn under a 2cm (¾in) fold on other edge of lap and stitch over seam on the outside.

4. On the inside, bring edges together and stitch diagonally across lower edge. (Fig 4.10)

Fig 4.10 On the inside, bring edges together and stitch diagonally across lower edge.

5. Press left edge of lap to the inside.

6. Machine side seams of skirt. (Fig 4.11) Overlock seams and press towards the back.

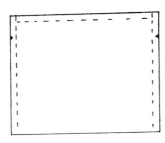

Fig 4.11 Machine side seams of skirt, and machine a gathering stitch on waistline.

7. Machine side seams of petticoat and back seam, leaving seam open above notch. Overlock seams and press flat open.

8. Machine a gathering stitch along top seam line of skirt and petticoat (Fig 4.11).

9. Pull up gathering stitch in sections to fit waistline of bodice.

10. With wrong sides of skirt and petticoat facing together, pin, tack and machine at waistline.

11. On right side of bodice and above piping, pin bodice to skirt matching side, centre front and centre back seams. (Change to a zipper foot and sew close to piping edge.)

Ruffle

1. Join seams of skirt ruffle. Overlock raw edges and press flat open.

2. Overlock bottom edge of ruffle. Press upwards and machine close to edge.

3. Machine a gathering stitching along top seam of ruffle. Pull up gathering in sections to fit bottom of skirt.

4. Pin, tack and machine ruffle to skirt, matching side seams of skirt to seams of ruffle and distributing gathers evenly. Overlock seam edge. (Fig 4.12)

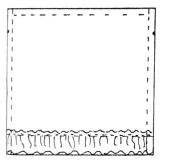

Fig 4.12 Machine ruffle to skirt.

5. Repeat Step 4 with taffeta frill for petticoat.

6. Pin and tack eyelet lace over ruffle seam. Machine each side of eyelet section.

Sleeves

Refer to Sleeves on page 102

1. At bottom edge of sleeve, fold broken line to solid line where pattern indicates. (Fig 4.13) Repeat with lining. With right sides of sleeve and lining facing together, pin, tack and machine across bottom of sleeve. Turn sleeve to right side and press.

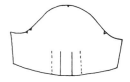

Fig 4.13 Fold broken line to solid line on sleeve.

2. Machine side seam of sleeve and press flat open. Machine side seam of lining and press flat open, with each seam facing together.

3. Machine a gathering stitch on seam between front and two back notches. (Fig 4.14)

Fig 4.14 Machine underarm seam and a gathering stitch at top of sleeve.

4. With right sides facing each other, drop sleeve into armhole and match notches. Pin, tack and machine sleeve armhole seams. Overlock seams. Repeat the above steps for second sleeve.

5. Machine zip into back opening. *Refer to Setting in a Zip on page 100.*

Bows

1. Cut three strips of black ribbon 12.5cm (5in) long to make bows. Mark the centre of each bow and fold ends towards the back.

2. Stitch in place and pull into the centre.

3. Cut three 2.5cm (1in) strips and pin one over the centre of each bow. Hand-stitch at the back.

4. Pin one bow in the centre of each ribbon on bodice. Hand-stitch at the back. (4.15)

Fig 4.15 Machine in zip. Stitch a bow in the centre of each ribbon on bodice.

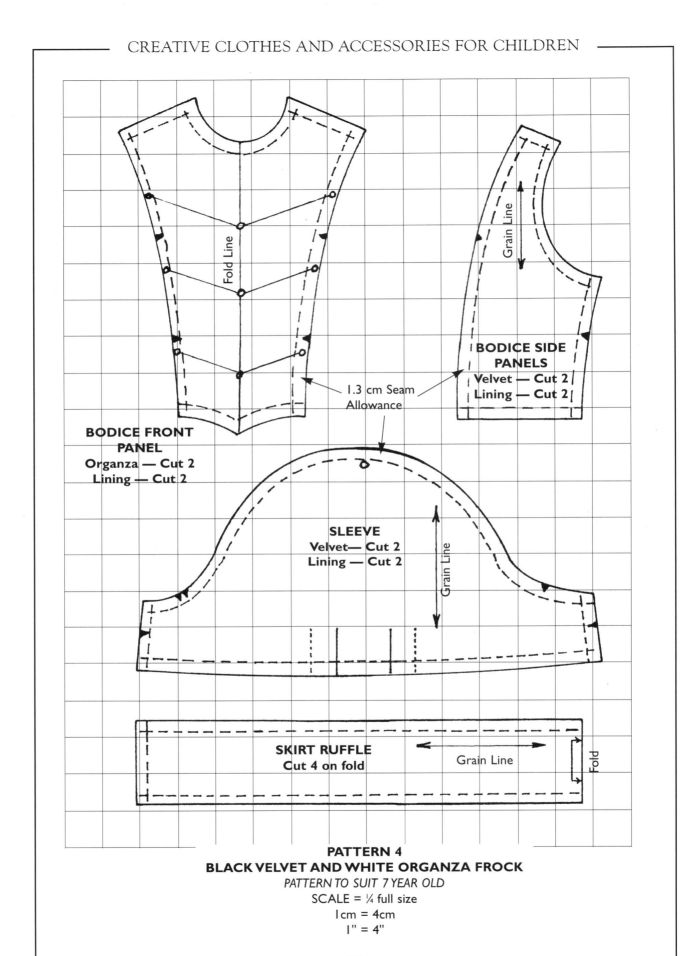

BODICE FRONT PANEL
Organza — Cut 2
Lining — Cut 2

Fold Line

1.3 cm Seam Allowance

BODICE SIDE PANELS
Velvet — Cut 2
Lining — Cut 2

Grain Line

SLEEVE
Velvet— Cut 2
Lining — Cut 2

Grain Line

SKIRT RUFFLE
Cut 4 on fold

Grain Line

Fold

PATTERN 4
BLACK VELVET AND WHITE ORGANZA FROCK
PATTERN TO SUIT 7 YEAR OLD
SCALE = ¼ full size
1cm = 4cm
1" = 4"

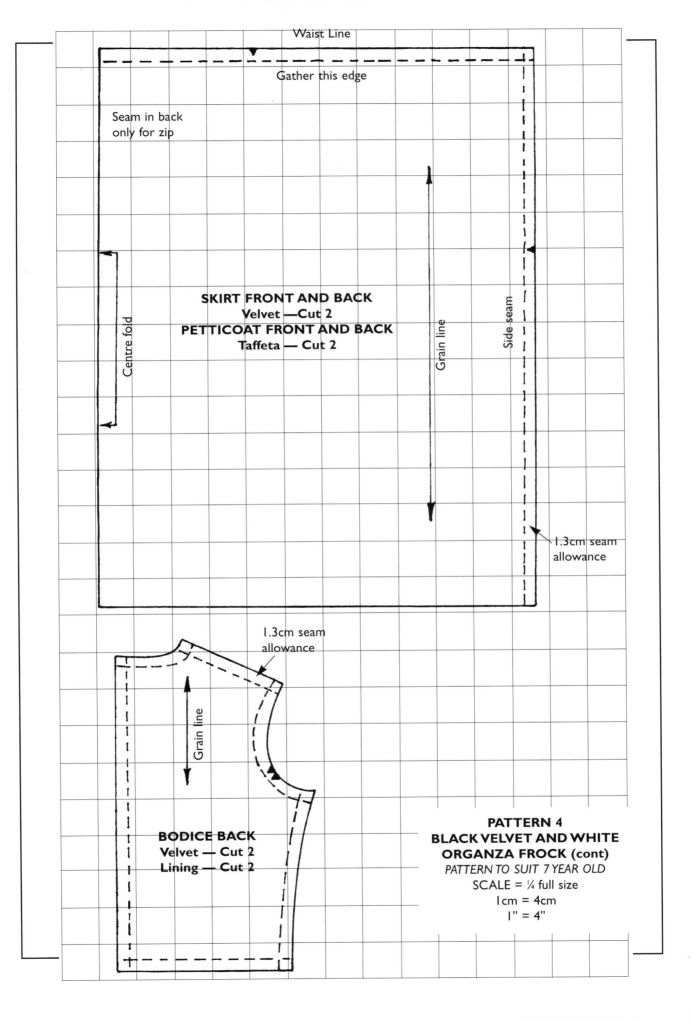

Waist Line

Gather this edge

Seam in back
only for zip

Centre fold

Grain line

Side seam

SKIRT FRONT AND BACK
Velvet —Cut 2
PETTICOAT FRONT AND BACK
Taffeta — Cut 2

1.3cm seam
allowance

1.3cm seam
allowance

Grain line

BODICE BACK
Velvet — Cut 2
Lining — Cut 2

**PATTERN 4
BLACK VELVET AND WHITE
ORGANZA FROCK (cont)**
PATTERN TO SUIT 7 YEAR OLD
SCALE = ¼ full size
1cm = 4cm
1" = 4"

5. BUCCANEER SHIRT AND TROUSERS

Boys like to look as modern as girls for that special occasion. This buccaneer shirt made of white polyester cloth and teamed with black cotton trousers gives a swashbuckling effect.

Pattern designed to fit 5 year old

MATERIALS

    1.4m (1½yd) of 115cm (45in) wide white polyester material

    2m (2⅛yd) of 115cm (45in) wide black poplin material

    23cm (¼yd) iron-on interfacing

    90cm (1yd) white silk cording

    4 white covered buttons

    1 reel white polyester thread

    1 reel black polyester thread

    90cm (1yd) of 2.5cm (1in) wide black elastic

METHOD

Shirt

1. Machine back bodice to front at shoulders. Overlock seams and press towards the back. (Fig 5.1)

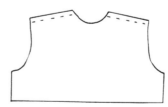

Fig 5.1 Machine back to front at shoulders.

2. Machine a rouleau 30.5cm (12in) in length and cut into 8 strips. *Refer to Rouleaus on page 104.*

3. On each side of neck opening, pin rouleaus in place where pattern indicates, ie. 14mm (½in) apart with loops facing towards armholes. (Fig 5.2)

4. Press seam over to wrong side at top of neck facing. With right sides together, pin facing to front around neckline, and all around rouleaus at neck opening. Tack and machine.

Fig 5.2 Pin rouleaus in place. Press seam over at top of facing.

5. Clip around neck and neck opening. Turn facing to wrong side and press flat. Overlock raw edges.

Collar

Fig 5.3 Iron interfacing to collar section.

1. Press iron-on facing to wrong side of collar section. (Fig 5.3)
2. With right sides facing each other, machine collar sections together leaving notched edge open. Trim seam and cut away bulk diagonally at corners. (Fig 5.4) Turn collar to right side and press flat. (Fig 5.5)

Fig 5.4 With right sides facing, machine collar sections together. Cut bulk from corners.

Fig 5.5 Turn collar to right side. Press flat.

3. On right side of neck edge and (facing side only) of collar, tack and machine together. Clip seam and press towards collar. (Fig 5.6)
4. Fold under remaining edge of collar onto neckline seam. Tack and machine close to the edge. (Fig 5.7)

Fig 5.6 On right side of neck edge and (facing side only) of collar, machine together.

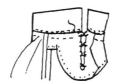

Fig 5.7 Fold under remaining edge of collar onto neckline seam and machine close to the edge.

Placket

1. Cut a bias binding strip 35cm (14in) long and 2.5cm (1in) wide.
2. Machine a 'V'-shaped row of stitching on seam line where opening is to be cut in sleeve. Cut to end of opening.
3. With right sides of sleeve and binding facing together, pin and tack along placket opening. Machine and press seam flat.

4. Fold binding to wrong side encasing raw edges. Fold edge of binding to meet stitching line. Pin in place, then tack and machine close to the edge. (Fig 5.8)

5. Turn binding to wrong side of sleeve and press placket flat. (Fig 5.9) Repeat the steps above for second sleeve.

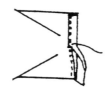

Fig 5.8   Fold edge of binding on placket and machine.

Fig 5.9   Press placket flat.

Cuffs

1. Cut iron-on interfacing half the depth of the cuff. Press in place on wrong side.

2. Fold cuff in half, right sides together.

3. At right-hand end, machine down 5cm (2in) then across 2.5cm (1in) to make the buttonhole section. Trim seam and cut seam corners diagonally to remove bulk.

4. Machine seam at end of cuff.

5. At end of overlap (buttonhole) section, cut up a little and turn cuff to right side. Press flat.

6. Pin right side of cuff to wrong side of sleeve. Tack, machine and trim seam. (Fig 5.10)

Fig 5.10 Machine cuff to sleeve. Fold under remaining raw edge and machine.

7. Fold and press seam on edge of cuff seam and top stitch. Repeat the steps above for second cuff.

Setting in the Sleeve

1. With right sides together, pin sleeve to armhole edge matching centre front and two back notches. (Fig 5.11) Tack and machine. Press seam towards shirt. Overlock seam edges. Repeat for second sleeve. *Refer to Sleeves on page 102.*

Fig 5.11 Pin sleeve to armhole edge.

2. Pin back to front at sides, pinning sleeve edges together. Machine in continuous seams along seam line. Overlock edges. (Fig 5.12)

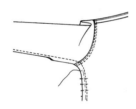

Fig 5.12 Machine side seams in a continuous seam.

3. Press up a 14mm (½in) hem on bottom edge of shirt. Machine close to the edge.

4. Machine a buttonhole in each cuff section. Sew a button at the centre of each buttonhole. (Fig 5.13)

Fig 5.13 Thread cording through neck loops. Stitch buttons in place.

5. Thread cording through neck loops long enough to make ties.

Buccaneer Trousers

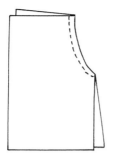

Fig 5.14 Machine two back pants sections together down centre back seam. Repeat with fronts.

1. With right sides facing each other, pin and tack the two back sections together down centre back seam. (Fig 5.14) Trim seam and overlock edges. Press seam to one side.

2. Repeat with front sections.

3. With right sides together, pin front to back down inside and outside legs and machine. (Fig 5.15) Machine the front and the back side seams together. Overlock edges and press seams flat.

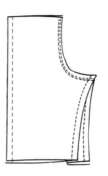

Fig 5.15 Machine front to back at inside leg seams.

4. Fold waistline down 2.5cm (1in) to the inside to make casing for elastic. Pin in place leaving a 2.5cm (1in) opening at centre front to thread elastic. (Fig 5.16)

5. Pin one end of elastic through a large safety pin and thread elastic through casing, adjusting to a comfortable fit. Hand-stitch ends of elastic and machine close the opening.

6. Fold up and press a 2.5cm (1in) hem on trousers. Machine close to the edge. (Fig 5.16)

Fig 5.16 Machine a 2.5cm (1in) casing at waistline. Thread elastic through casing. Machine a 2.5cm (1in) hem on bottom of trousers.

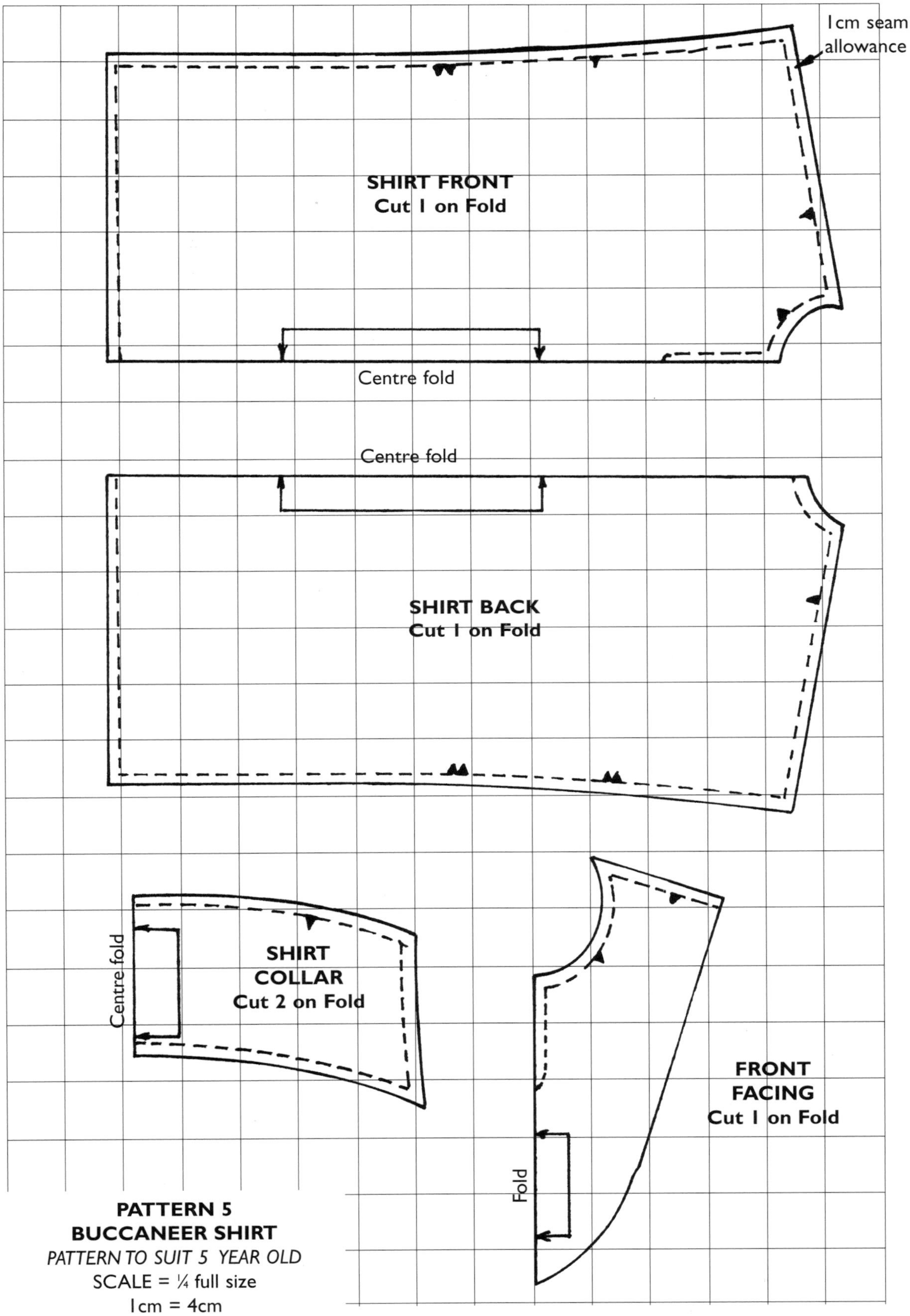

1cm seam
allowance

SHIRT FRONT
Cut 1 on Fold

Centre fold

Centre fold

SHIRT BACK
Cut 1 on Fold

Centre fold

**SHIRT
COLLAR**
Cut 2 on Fold

Fold

**FRONT
FACING**
Cut 1 on Fold

**PATTERN 5
BUCCANEER SHIRT**
PATTERN TO SUIT 5 YEAR OLD
SCALE = ¼ full size
1cm = 4cm
1" = 4"

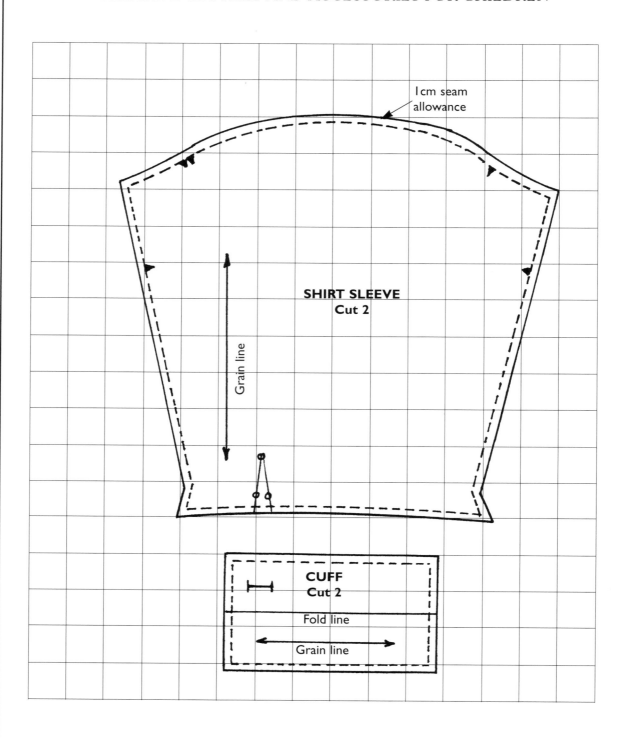

1cm seam
allowance

SHIRT SLEEVE
Cut 2

Grain line

CUFF
Cut 2

Fold line

Grain line

PATTERN 5
BUCCANEER SHIRT (cont)
PATTERN TO SUIT 5 YEAR OLD
SCALE = ¼ full size
1cm = 4cm
1" = 4"

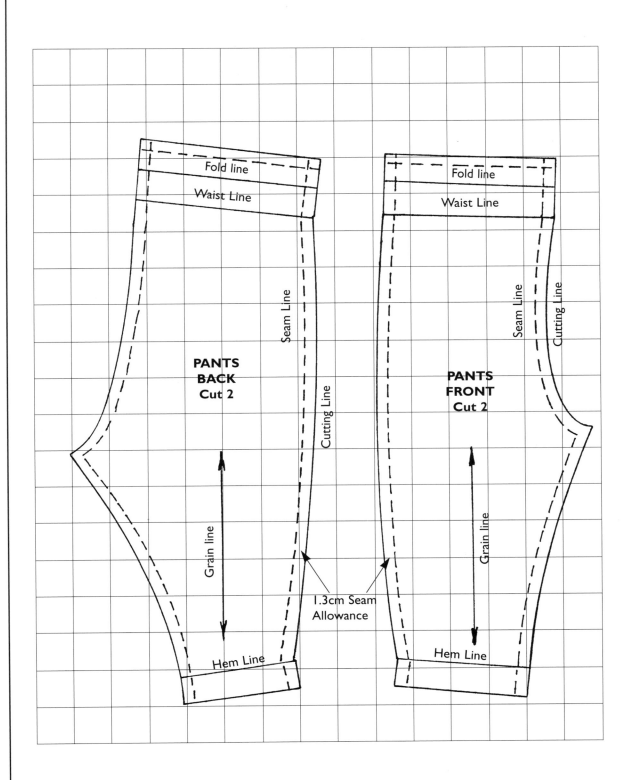

Fold line

Waist Line

Seam Line

Cutting Line

**PANTS
BACK
Cut 2**

Grain line

Hem Line

Fold line

Waist Line

Seam Line

Cutting Line

**PANTS
FRONT
Cut 2**

Grain line

Hem Line

1.3cm Seam
Allowance

**PATTERN 5
BUCCANEER SHIRT (cont)**
PATTERN TO SUIT 5 YEAR OLD
SCALE = ¼ full size
1cm = 4cm
1" = 4"

6. SATIN SHORTIE PYJAMAS

What could be more chic than satin shortie pyjamas with a heart-shaped pocket full of dreams.

Pattern designed to fit 4 year old

MATERIALS

    2.6m (2⅞yd) of 115cm (45in) wide satin material

    1 reel of matching polyester thread

    70cm (¾yd) of 2.5cm (1in) wide elastic

    3 matching covered buttons

METHOD

Top

1. With right sides of pocket facing together, pin, tack and machine around edge of seam line leaving an opening between dots. Clip seam and turn to right side through the opening. Press flat. Hand-slip opening closed. (Figs 6.1 and 6.2)

Fig 6.1 Stitch pocket between dots, right sides facing. Clip around edge.

Fig 6.2 Turn pocket to right side. Stitch opening closed.

2. On right side of front, pin pocket on pocket line marking. (Fig 6.3) Tack and machine close to edge along lower section.

Fig 6.3 Stitch pocket to right front on pocket marking.

3. Machine front to back at shoulders. (Fig 6.4) Overlock seams and press towards the back.

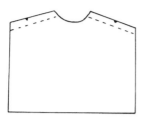

Fig 6.4 Stitch front to back at shoulder seams.

4. Cut down on collar to small 'o's. (Fig 6.5) Turn in seam allowance of collar between clips. (Fig 6.6) Press.

Fig 6.5 Cut down on collar to small 'o's.

Fig 6.6 Turn in seam allowance of collar between clips.

5. Machine collar sections together leaving notched edge open. (Fig 6.7) Trim and clip seam.

6. Pin collar to neck edge matching centre backs and notches. (Fig 6.8) Tack and machine. Trim and clip seam.

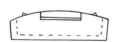

Fig 6.7 Stitch collar sections together leaving notched edge open.

Fig 6.8 Pin collar to neck edge.

7. With right sides together, pin facing to front and neck edge. (Fig 6.9) Tack and machine. Trim seams and corners. Clip curves.

Fig 6.9 Pin facing to front and neck edge.

8. Turn facing to inside, turning back seam towards collar. Press. Stitch pressed edge of collar over neck edge. (Fig 6.10)

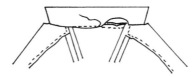

Fig 6.10 Stitch pressed edge of collar over neck edge.

9. With right sides facing together, pin sleeve to armhole edge matching front and two back notches. Tack and machine. Trim seam and overlock edges. Press seam towards sleeve. Repeat for second sleeve. *Refer to Sleeves on page 102.*

10. Pin front to back at underarm seams, matching armhole seams. Trim seams and overlock. Press seams towards the back.

11. Press up 6mm (¼in) hem on raw edges of sleeves and bottom of top.

12. Using the pattern as a guide, place it along finished edge of garment and transfer buttonhole markings to left front of garment. Machine buttonholes at markings, lap left front over right front, matching centres. Sew buttons under buttonholes.

Pants

1. Machine pants front to pants back at inside leg edges. (Fig 6.11) Overlock seams.

Fig 6.11 Machine pants front to pants back at inside leg edges.

2. Machine centre seam matching inside leg seams. (Fig 6.12) Overlock seams.

Fig 6.12 Machine centre seam matching inside leg seams.

3. Pin back to front at sides. Machine and overlock seams. (Fig 6.13) Press seams towards the back.

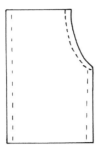

Fig 6.13 Pin back to front at sides and machine.

4. To make casing for elastic, turn down 3cm (1¼in) along upper edge of garment. Tack close to fold and press. (Fig 6.14)

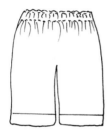

Fig 6.14 Machine casing along upper edge. Insert elastic to fit waist.

5. Turn under 6mm (¼in) on raw edge and machine in place leaving an opening to insert elastic through casing. Lap ends of elastic 14mm (½in) over each other then tack and machine together. Machine opening of casing closed.

6. Turn up a 6mm (¼in) hem on lower edges of pants and press. Turn under 6mm (¼in) on raw edges and machine in place.

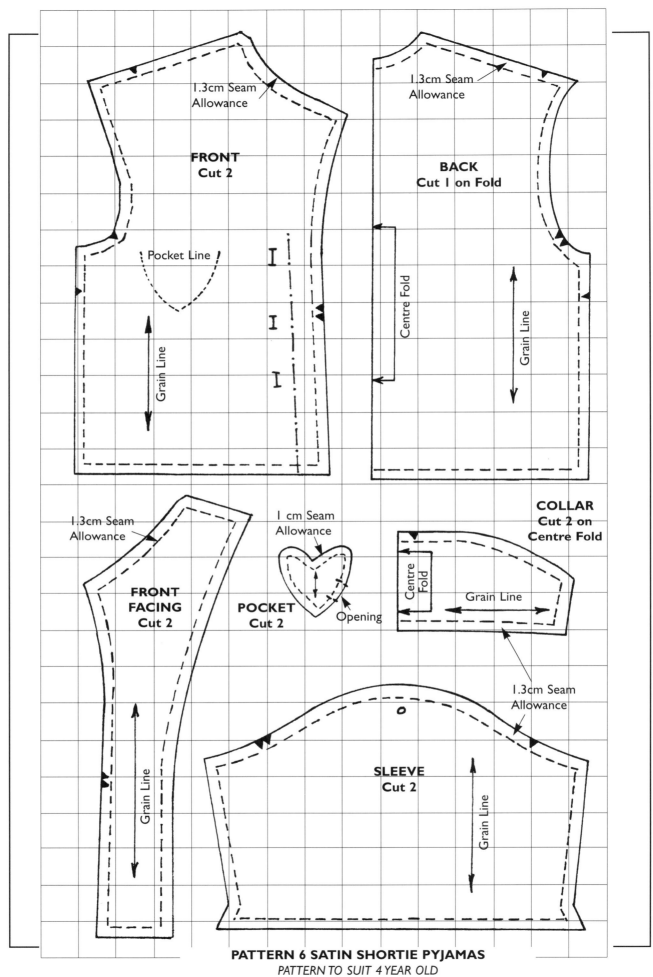

FRONT
Cut 2

1.3cm Seam Allowance

Pocket Line

Grain Line

BACK
Cut 1 on Fold

1.3cm Seam Allowance

Centre Fold

Grain Line

FRONT FACING
Cut 2

1.3cm Seam Allowance

Grain Line

POCKET
Cut 2

1 cm Seam Allowance

Opening

COLLAR
Cut 2 on Centre Fold

Centre Fold

Grain Line

1.3cm Seam Allowance

SLEEVE
Cut 2

Grain Line

PATTERN 6 SATIN SHORTIE PYJAMAS
PATTERN TO SUIT 4 YEAR OLD
SCALE = ¼ full size 1cm = 4cm 1" = 4"

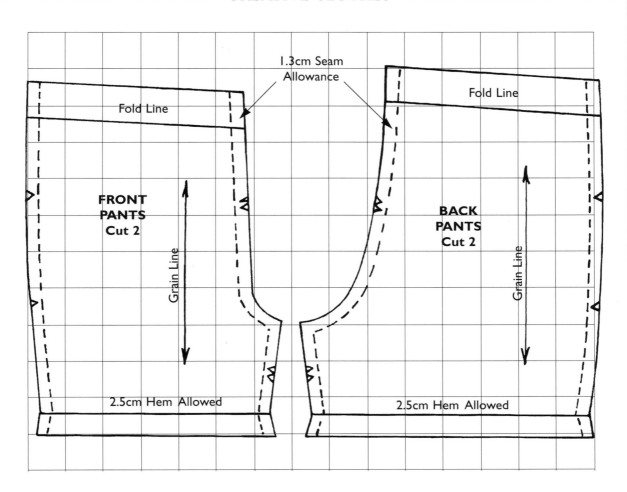

PATTERN 6 SATIN SHORTIE PYJAMAS (cont)
PATTERN TO SUIT 4 YEAR OLD
SCALE = ¼ full size
1cm = 4cm
1" = 4"

Clothes for Page Boys and Flower Girls

7. SILK AND TULLE FLOWER GIRL FROCK

Little girls always love being part of a wedding, especially when chosen to be the very important flower girl.

This frock has a cream silk bodice with frothy puff sleeves, two gathered tulle skirts with matching silk underskirt and fluted hemlines. Trimmings include a lace edging with velvet pink ribbon, and soft pink cloth roses which decorate the sleeves.

Pattern designed to fit 5 year old

MATERIALS

    1.6m (1¾yd) cream raw silk

    1.4m (1½yd) matching taffeta (for petticoat)

    2.3m (2½yd) cream silk tulle

    3.66m (4yd) of 5cm (2in) wide ribbon frill

    50cm (20in) of soft pink raw silk (for cloth roses)

    30.5cm (12in) zip

    1 reel matching polyester thread.

METHOD

1. Machine shoulder seams of bodice. Repeat with lining. (Fig 7.1) Press seams flat open.

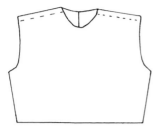

Fig 7.1 Machine shoulder seams of bodice. Repeat with lining.

2. With right sides of bodice and lining facing together, pin, tack and machine around neckline and down the two back sections (where zip will be machined). (Fig 7.2)

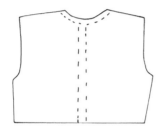

Fig 7.2 Machine bodice and lining together.

3. Cut a strip of the ribbon frill long enough to fit neck edge and allowing for a 14mm (½in) fold at each end. Pin, tack and machine frill to neck edge. (Fig 7.3)

4. Machine side seams of bodice. Repeat with lining. Press seams flat.

5. Machine side seams, and back seam of petticoat to circle. Neaten seams and press flat. Machine seams of the two tulle skirts. (Fig 7.4)

Fig 7.3 Machine ribbon frill onto neckline. Machine side seams of bodice.

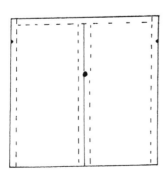

Fig 7.4 Machine side seams and back seams of skirts. Gather up waistlines.

6. Machine a gathering stitch along top seam of each skirt. Pull up gathering stitch on petticoat to fit waist area of bodice. Pin one tulle skirt onto petticoat distributing gathers evenly. Tack and machine. Pin second tulle skirt on top of the other. Tack and machine.

7. With right sides of bodice and skirt facing each other, pin, tack and machine together. (Fig 7.5) Trim seam and overlock edges.

Fig 7.5 Machine bodice to skirt, and machine in zip. Machine ribbon frill onto waistline.

8. Machine zip in place. *Refer to Setting in a Zip on page 100.*

9. Measure waist area and cut the ribbon frill to fit waist allowing for a 14mm (½in) fold at each end. Pin, tack and machine centre of frill to waistline.

10. Machine a gathering stitch along top of sleeve seam between front and two back notches. Run a gathering stitch along bottom edge of sleeve. (Fig 7.6) Pull gathering up to fit arm comfortably. Measure the distance around the arm and cut two strips of ribbon frill to fit. Machine centre of frill to edge of sleeve. (Fig 7.7) Machine side seams of sleeves and overlock edges. (Fig 7.8) Machine sleeves into armholes. *Refer to Sleeves on page 102.*

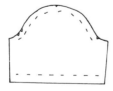

Fig 7.6 Machine a gathering stitch at the top of each sleeve and along the bottom edge.

Fig 7.7 Machine ribbon frill to edge of sleeves.

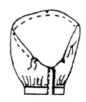

Fig 7.8 Machine seams of sleeves and overlock edges.

11. Level hemlines of all three skirts and flute edges. *Refer to Fluting Edges on page 108.*

12. Sew six cloth roses from the pink raw silk material. Hand-stitch three on the centre bottom of each sleeve. (Fig 7.9) *Refer to Cloth Roses on page 96.*

Fig 7.9 Machine sleeves into armholes. Flute hemlines of skirt. Make six cloth roses and sew three in the middle of each sleeve.

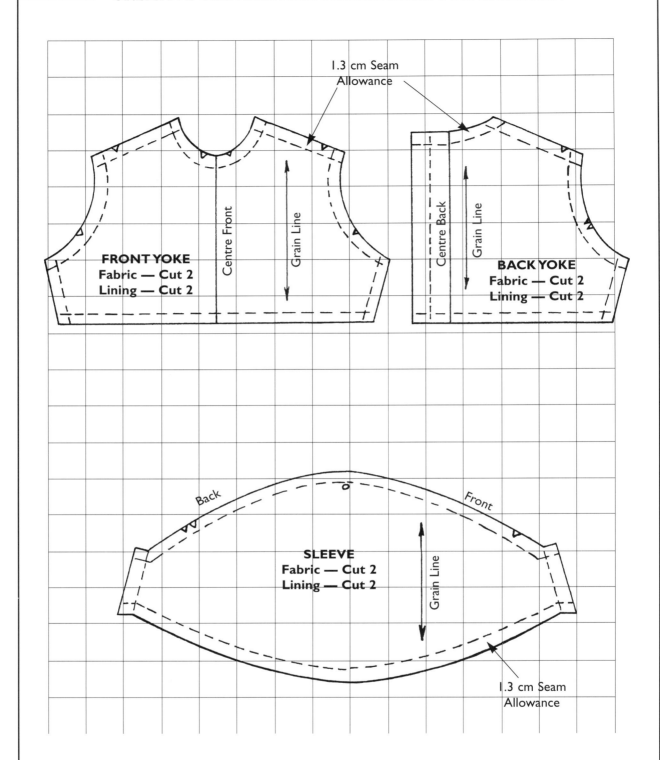

PATTERN 7
SILK AND TULLE FLOWER GIRL FROCK
PATTERN TO SUIT 5 YEAR OLD
SCALE = ¼ full size
1cm = 4cm
1" = 4"

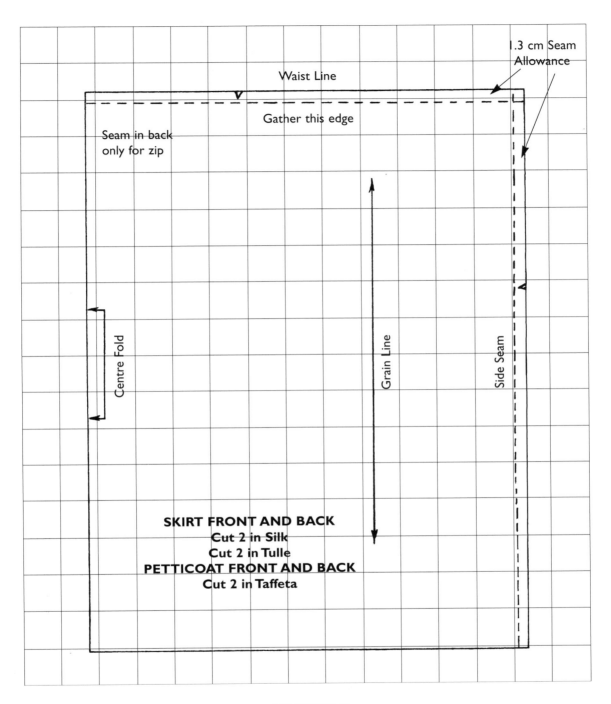

Waist Line

Gather this edge

Seam in back
only for zip

1.3 cm Seam
Allowance

Centre Fold

Grain Line

Side Seam

SKIRT FRONT AND BACK
Cut 2 in Silk
Cut 2 in Tulle
PETTICOAT FRONT AND BACK
Cut 2 in Taffeta

PATTERN 7
SILK AND TULLE FLOWER GIRL FROCK (cont)
PATTERN TO SUIT 5 YEAR OLD
SCALE = ¼ full size
1cm = 4cm
1" = 4"

8. RAW SILK FLOWER GIRL FROCK

Pattern designed to fit 3 year old

MATERIALS

    2.75m (3yd) of 115cm (45in) wide cream raw silk

    2.3m (2 ½yd) of 115cm (45in) wide cream taffeta for petticoat

    50cm (20in) strip of pale pink raw silk for roses

    1 reel matching polyester thread

    28cm (11in) zip

METHOD

1.   Machine shoulder seams of bodice. (Fig 8.1) Press flat. Repeat with lining.

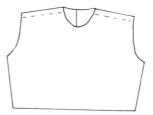

Fig 8.1 Machine shoulder seams of bodice and lining.

2.   With wrong sides facing each other, baste bodice and lining together. (Fig 8.2)

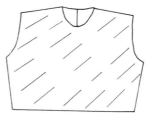

Fig 8.2 Baste bodice and lining together. Machine a binding onto neckline.

Fig 8.3 Flute curved edges of the four ruffles.

3.   Measure neck area of bodice adding 4cm (1½in) for a seam allowance. Cut on the bias a strip of the raw silk material this length and 6.25cm (2½in) wide and machine a binding on the neck. *Refer to Bindings on page 106.*

4.   Flute curved edges of the four ruffles. (Fig 8.3) *Refer to Fluting Edges on page 108.*

5.   Machine side seams of bodice. Neaten edges and press flat. (Fig 8.4)

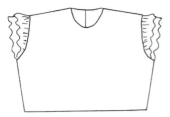

Fig 8.4 Machine side seams of bodice. Machine ruffles to armholes and a binding on waistline.

6.   Machine a gathering stitch on straight-edged seam of each ruffle. Pull up gathering thread and pin one ruffle in each armhole between front notch and two back notches. Tack and machine. Repeat with other two frills. Pin one frill on top of the other. Overlock armhole seams.

7.   Press zip seam of back bodice flat open.

8.   Measure waistline of bodice and machine a binding to the edge the same as with neckline. Refer to Step 3.

9.   Machine skirt back sections together leaving opening for zip at circle. Repeat for petticoat. Machine skirt side seams. Repeat for petticoat.

10. Machine a gathering stitch along upper edges of skirt and petticoat. With wrong sides of skirt and petticoat facing each other, pin centres and side seams together. Pull up gathering and evenly distribute gathers to fit waistline.

11. Pin and tack bodice to skirt. (Fig 8.5) Change machine foot to a zipper foot and machine in the ditch on the piping.

Fig 8.5 Machine seams on skirt and petticoat. Machine bodice to skirt. Machine zip in back. Hand-stitch a bow to top of each sleeve. Hand-stitch a cluster of roses to waistline.

12. Machine zip in back opening. *Refer to Setting in a Zip on page 100.*

13. Press up a 6.25cm (2½in) hem on skirt and petticoat. Machine close to hem edges.

14. Next make the shoulder bows. With right sides of bow strips facing together, machine on seam line. Pin a safety pin to one end and pull through to right side. Fold ends, lapping 14mm (½in) to the centre. Hand-stitch together. Cut a 4cm (1½in) length strip, press a 6mm (¼in) fold each side and wrap over centre of bow, stitching at the back. Hand-stitch a bow to the top of each sleeve. (Fig 8.6)

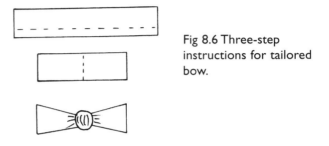

Fig 8.6 Three-step instructions for tailored bow.

15. Make five tiny cloth roses, group them together and hand-stitch to waistline. *Refer to Cloth Roses on page 96.*

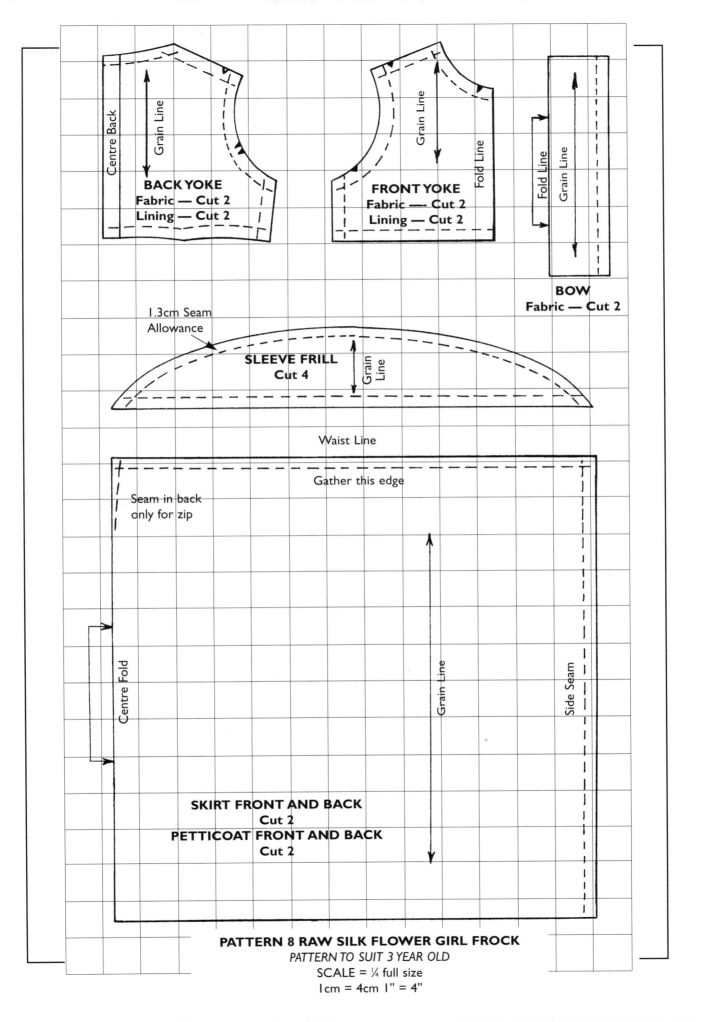

BACK YOKE
Fabric — Cut 2
Lining — Cut 2

Centre Back

Grain Line

FRONT YOKE
Fabric — Cut 2
Lining — Cut 2

Grain Line

Fold Line

BOW
Fabric — Cut 2

Fold Line

Grain Line

1.3cm Seam Allowance

SLEEVE FRILL
Cut 4

Grain Line

Waist Line

Gather this edge

Seam in back only for zip

Centre Fold

Grain Line

Side Seam

SKIRT FRONT AND BACK
Cut 2
PETTICOAT FRONT AND BACK
Cut 2

PATTERN 8 RAW SILK FLOWER GIRL FROCK
PATTERN TO SUIT 3 YEAR OLD
SCALE = ¼ full size
1cm = 4cm 1" = 4"

9. PAGE BOY SUIT

The page boy suit is made from cream raw silk to compliment the flower girl frock.

Pattern designed to fit 5 year old

MATERIALS

2m (2¼yd) of 115cm (45in) wide raw silk
1m (1⅛yd) matching taffeta for jacket lining
5 covered buttons
1 reel matching polyester thread
1m (1⅛yd) of 2.5cm (1in) wide non-roll elastic

METHOD

Jacket

1. Machine front to back at shoulders. Repeat with lining. (Fig 9.1) Press seams together towards the back.

Fig 9.1 Machine front to back at shoulders. Repeat with lining.

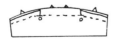

Fig 9.2 Machine 1.5cm (⅝in) from notched edge on one collar section. Clip to small dots.

2. Machine 1.5cm (⅝in) from notched edge on one collar section. Clip notched edge of collar to small dots. (Fig 9.2)

3. Press under 1.5cm (⅝in) on raw edge between clips. Trim to 6mm (¼in). With right sides together, machine facing to collar leaving notched edge open. Trim seams and corners. (Fig 9.3)

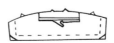

Fig 9.3 Press under 1.5cm (⅝in) on edge between clips. Machine facing to collar leaving notched edge open. Trim seams and corners.

4. Turn collar to right side. Press flat. (Fig 9.4)

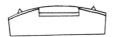

Fig 9.4 Turn collar to right side. Press flat.

5. Clip neck edge on the outside. Pin collar (facing side) to neck edges matching centre back. Tack collar and facing sections to neck edge between small dots. (Fig 9.5)

Fig 9.5 Pin collar facing to neck edge. Tack collar facing sections to neck edge between small dots.

6. Overlock edge of front facing. Clip neck edge. With right sides together, pin and tack facing to front and neck edges and machine. Trim corners. (Fig 9.6)

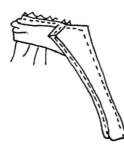

Fig 9.6 With right sides facing together, machine facing to front and neck edge. Trim corners.

7. Turn facing to the inside and press back neck seam towards collar. Machine pressed edge of collar over neck seam. (Fig 9.7)

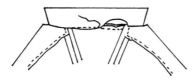

Fig 9.7 Turn facing to inside. Machine pressed edge of collar over neck seam.

8. With right sides together, pin sleeves to armholes matching notches. Tack and machine. Overlock edges.

9. Pin front to back at underarm seams and machine. Press seams towards the back and overlock edges.

10. Press up a 4cm (1½in) hem along bottom of jacket and hand-slip in place.

11. Drop cuff into sleeve and with wrong side of sleeve and right side of cuff facing together, tack and machine. Fold and press cuff to right side of sleeve. Repeat for second sleeve.

12. Mark and machine buttonholes evenly on left-hand side of jacket. Hand-stitch buttons in the centre of each button hole.

Jacket Lining

1. Machine front and back lining sections together at shoulders. (Fig 9.8) Press seams towards the back.

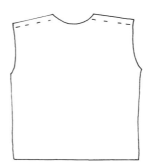

Fig 9.8 Machine front and back of lining at shoulder seams.

2. On seam line at top of sleeves, machine a gathering stitch between notches (to help mould the sleeves in place). (Fig 9.9) *Refer to Sleeves on page 102.*

Fig 9.9 Machine a gathering stitch along top of sleeves. Machine sleeves in armholes.

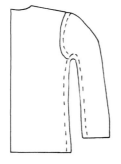

Fig 9.10 Machine front to back at entire underarm seam.

3. With right sides of jacket and lining facing together, pin sleeves to armhole edges, matching notches. Tack in place and machine. Press seams towards bottom of sleeves.

4. Pin front to back along entire underarm seams matching armhole seams. (Fig 9.10) Press seams towards the back.

5. With right sides of jacket and lining facing together, pin edge of lining to edge of jacket. (Fig 9.11) Tack and machine. Clip curves and press. Turn jacket to right side and drop sleeve linings into jacket sleeves.

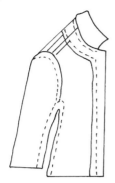

Fig 9.11 With right sides of jacket and lining facing together, pin edge of lining to edge of jacket.

6. Press up a 2.5cm (1in) hem at bottom of jacket and machine. Repeat with lining hem.

7. Machine hems on sleeves. (Fig 9.12) Hand-stitch lining to jacket at hemline of sleeves.

Fig 9.12 Machine hems of lining and sleeves.

Trousers

1. With right sides facing each other, pin, tack and machine the two back sections together down centre back. Trim seam and overlock edges. Press seam to one side. (Fig 9.13)

Fig 9.13 Machine two back sections together down centre back seam. Repeat with front sections.

2.   Repeat with front sections.
3.   With right sides together, pin and machine front to back down inside and outside legs. Machine the front and the back side seams together. Overlock edges and press seams flat. (Fig 9.14)

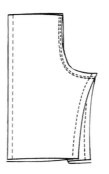

Fig 9.14 Machine front to back at inside legs.

4.   Fold waistline down 4cm (1½in) to the inside to make casing for elastic. Pin in place leaving a 2.5cm (1in) opening in centre front to thread elastic through. Machine close to the edge. (Fig 9.15)
5.   Fold up a 4cm (1½in) hem on trousers leaving a 2.5cm (1in) opening to thread elastic through. Machine close to the edge. (Fig 9.15)

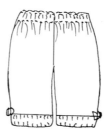

Fig 9.15 Machine casing at waistline and thread elastic through. Machine hems on bottom of trousers and thread elastic through.

6.   Using a safety pin, thread elastic through casing at waistline and adjust to a comfortable fit. Hand-stitch ends of elastic and machine close the opening.
7.   Thread elastic through casing of each trouser leg and adjust to a comfortable fit. Hand-stitch the ends of the elastic and machine close the openings.

Bows

1.   Fold each strip in half lengthwise, right sides together. Machine a 10mm (⅜in) seam and leave an opening at each end.

2. Fasten a safety pin at one end and pull strip through to right side. Press flat.

3. Fold each end of one strip to the centre and stitch with a needle and thread.

4. Cut two strips of material, 7.5cm (3in) long by 7.5cm (3in) wide, to make centres of bows. Press each side of the strip 6mm (¼in) over. Cut in half and bind one around centre of bow. Stitch with a needle and thread at back of bow.

5. Pin a bow on each side seam of trousers above elastic casing. Stitch at back of bows.

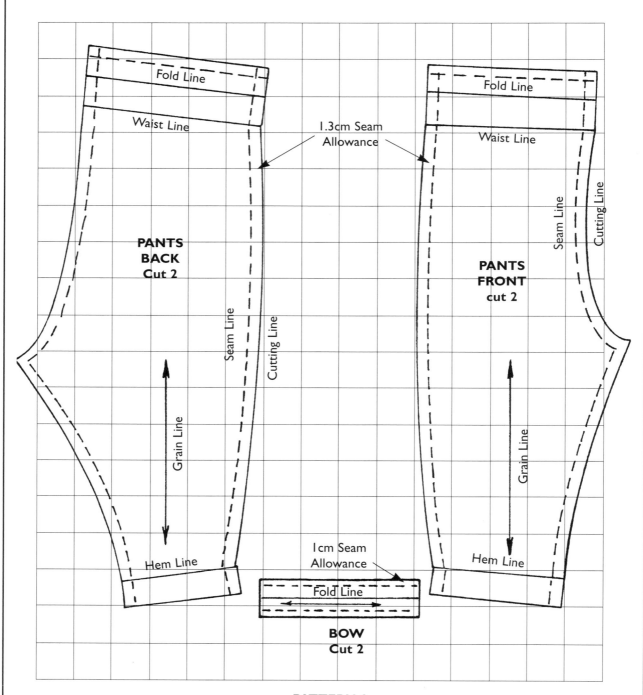

Fold Line

Waist Line

1.3cm Seam
Allowance

Fold Line

Waist Line

Seam Line

Cutting Line

**PANTS
BACK
Cut 2**

**PANTS
FRONT
cut 2**

Seam Line

Cutting Line

Grain Line

Grain Line

Hem Line

Hem Line

1cm Seam
Allowance

Fold Line

**BOW
Cut 2**

**PATTERN 9
PAGE BOY SUIT**
PATTERN TO SUIT 5 YEAR OLD
SCALE = ¼ full size
1cm = 4cm
1" = 4"

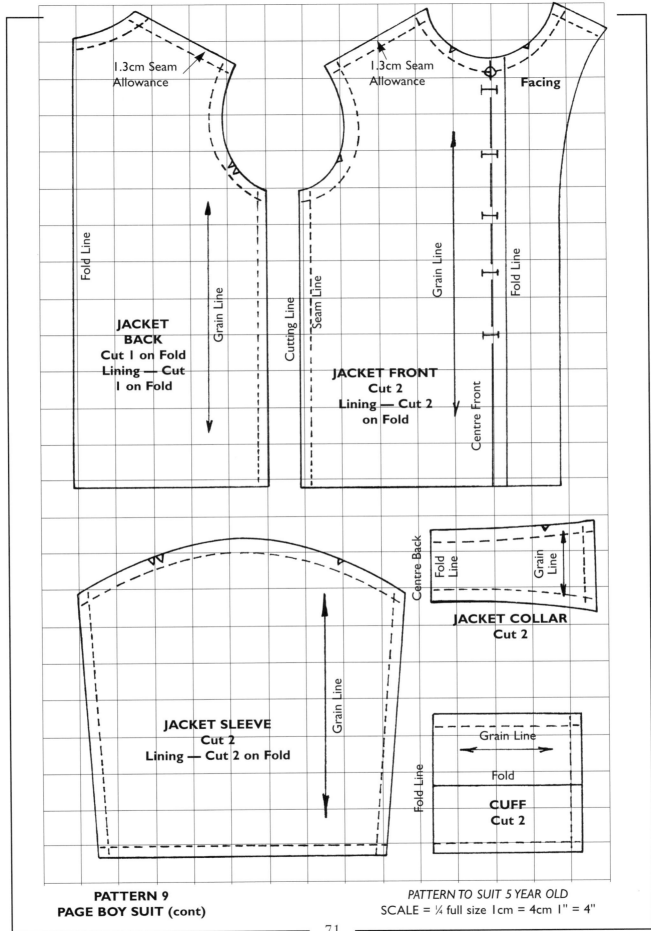

JACKET BACK
Cut 1 on Fold
Lining — Cut 1 on Fold

1.3cm Seam Allowance

Fold Line

Grain Line

Cutting Line

Seam Line

1.3cm Seam Allowance

Facing

Grain Line

Fold Line

Centre Front

JACKET FRONT
Cut 2
Lining — Cut 2 on Fold

Centre Back

Fold Line

Grain Line

JACKET COLLAR
Cut 2

JACKET SLEEVE
Cut 2
Lining — Cut 2 on Fold

Grain Line

Grain Line

Fold

Fold Line

CUFF
Cut 2

PATTERN 9
PAGE BOY SUIT (cont)

PATTERN TO SUIT 5 YEAR OLD
SCALE = ¼ full size 1cm = 4cm 1" = 4"

Fancy Dress Costumes

10. Flower Fairy Costume

A fairy costume is always a favourite with children. This costume is made from two squares of georgette material sewn together. The bodice is created by sewing rows of shirring, and the straps are formed from plaited rouleau strips. The hem is fluted, and handmade silk roses are attached to the skirt. The wings are made from net, and the headband is decorated with a butterfly and four silk roses.

MATERIALS

    2m (2⅛yd) cream chiffon (for frock)
    1m (1⅛yd) net (for wings)
    1m (1⅛yd) pink silk organza (for cloth roses)
    1 reel matching polyester thread
    2 craft butterflies
    1 headband
    Green leaves
    2 reels matching shirring elastic

METHOD

1. Press over a 2.5cm (1in) fold at top of front and back sections of the fabric. (Fig 10.1)
2. On right side of front and back sections, draw eight straight horizontal lines using a marking pencil and ruler. (Fig 10.1)
3. Wind elastic thread by hand on the bobbin, stretching it slightly until the bobbin is almost full. Thread top thread with a polyester cotton.

Fig 10.1 Press a fold over at top of front and back sections. Mark horizontal lines.

4.   Machine across each line, holding the fabric front and back. Secure the ends by pulling the needle thread through to underside of elastic. Tie ends securely.

5.   With front and back sections facing together, pin, tack and machine side seams. Neaten edges and press towards the back. (Fig 10.2)

Fig 10.2 Machine across lines with shirring elastic. Machine side seams.

6.   Flute hemline. *Refer to Fluting Edges on page 108.*

7.   Sew six rouleaus 28.5cm (11¼in) long for the straps. *Refer to Rouleaus on page 104.*

8.   Stitch three rouleaus together 14mm (½in) down from the top. Plait together leaving 14mm (½in) at the end. Stitch in place.

9.   Hand-stitch straps in place 6.25cm (2½in) from centre front and centre of back of top. (Fig 10.3)

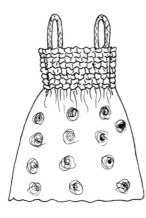

Fig 10.3 Flute hemline. Sew and hand-stitch straps in place. Make roses and stitch to skirt.

10.   Next make the cloth roses. Decide how many you will need for the front and back of the skirt and add four small roses for the headband. (Fig 10.8) *Refer to Cloth Roses on page 96.* Stitch roses to skirt.

Fig 10.8 Make four cloth roses. Glue roses and butterfly to headband.

Wings

1. Cut out a paper pattern 81cm (32in) long and 55cm (22in) wide. Pin onto net and cut out wings.
2. At top and bottom of the length, fold up 6.25cm (2½in) and pin in place. (Fig 10.4)

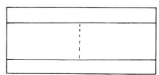

Fig 10.4 Pin fold over at top and bottom.

3. Fold both ends of the net to the centre and pin. (Fig 10.5)
4. With matching thread, hand-stitch two rows of running stitch in the centre of the length and leave a long thread at each end. (Fig 10.5)

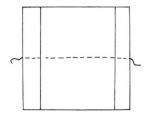

Fig 10.5 Bring both ends to the centre and hand-stitch a running stitch.

5. Pull threads and distribute gathers evenly. Tie off and cut thread ends. (Fig 10.6) Stitch securely in the centre.
6. Hand-stitch wings in place in centre of back bodice. (Fig 10.7)

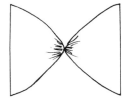

Fig 10.6 Pull up gathering stitch and tie off threads.

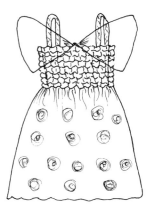

Fig 10.7 Hand-stitch wings to centre of back bodice.

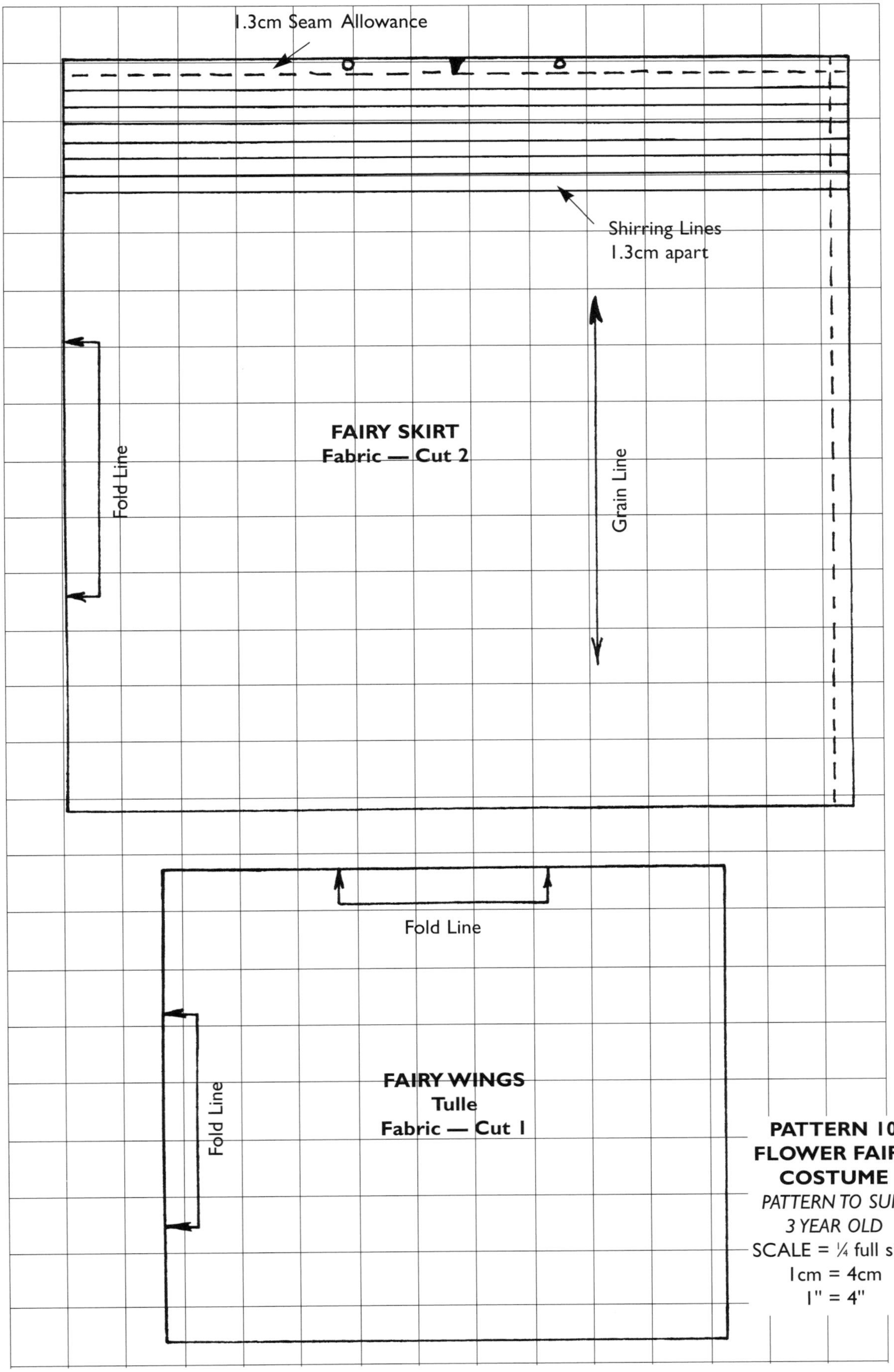

1.3cm Seam Allowance

Shirring Lines
1.3cm apart

Fold Line

Grain Line

FAIRY SKIRT
Fabric — Cut 2

Fold Line

FAIRY WINGS
Tulle
Fabric — Cut 1

Fold Line

PATTERN 10
FLOWER FAIRY
COSTUME
PATTERN TO SUIT
3 YEAR OLD
SCALE = ¼ full size
1cm = 4cm
1" = 4"

11. Purple and Jade Harem Costumes

Harem costumes are always a favourite, conjuring an atmosphere of far-off magical lands.

MATERIALS

    2.75m (3yd) chiffon (repeat for other colour)
    1m (1⅛yd) brocade
    90cm (1yd) taffeta (for lining)
    1.8m (2yd) of 2.5cm (1in) wide elastic
    1 reel matching polyester thread
    70cm (¾yd) velcro

METHOD

Pants

1. With right sides facing each other, pin, tack and machine the two back sections together down centre back seam. Overlock edges and press seam to one side. (Fig 11.1)
2. Repeat with front sections.
3. With right sides facing together, pin, tack and machine front to back down inside and outside legs. Overlock edges and press seams to one side. (Fig 11.2)

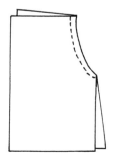 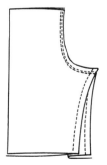

Fig 11.1 Machine two back sections together down centre back seam. Repeat with front sections.

Fig 11.2 Machine front to back at inside legs.

4. Press top down to make a 2.5cm (1in) casing for elastic. Pin in place leaving a 15cm (6in) opening in centre front to thread elastic through. (Fig 11.3)

Fig 11.3 Machine casing at waistline and thread elastic through. Repeat for bottom of pants.

5. Thread elastic through casing and adjust to a comfortable fit. Stitch opening closed.
6. Repeat these steps for elastic at bottom of pants.

Midriff

1. Pin, tack and machine shoulders of front section to shoulders of back bodice. (Fig 11.4) Repeat with lining. Press seams flat.

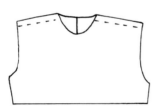

Fig 11.4 Machine front and back bodice sections at shoulders. Repeat with lining.

2. Pin, tack and machine side seams of front and back together. Repeat with lining. (Fig 11.5)
3. With wrong sides of front and lining facing each other, pin and baste together to become one top. (Fig 11.6)

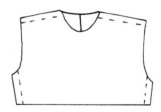

Fig 11.5 Machine side seams of midriff. Repeat with lining.

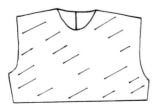

Fig 11.6 With wrong sides of midriff and lining facing, baste together to become one top.

4. Machine 'lama' bindings around neckline, armholes, hemline and the two back openings. (Fig 11.7) *Refer to Bindings on page 106.*

5. Machine velcro strips evenly down the two back openings. (Fig 11.8)

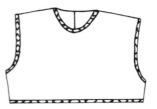

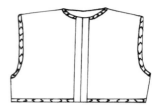

Fig 11.7 Machine lama bias bindings around neck, armholes, hemline and two back openings.

Fig 11.8 Machine velcro strips evenly down two back openings

Cummerbund (Fig 11.9)

1. With right sides of cummerbund and lining facing each other, pin, tack and machine together leaving a 15cm (6in) opening. Trim seams and turn out to right side. Cover material with a pressing cloth and press. Hand-stitch opening closed.

2. Machine a row of top stitching 6mm (¼in) from edge all the way around.

3. Repeat these steps for cummerbund with extended front piece. Hand-stitch the two pieces together under point section of cummerbund.

Fig 11.9 Machine lining to cummerbund sections.

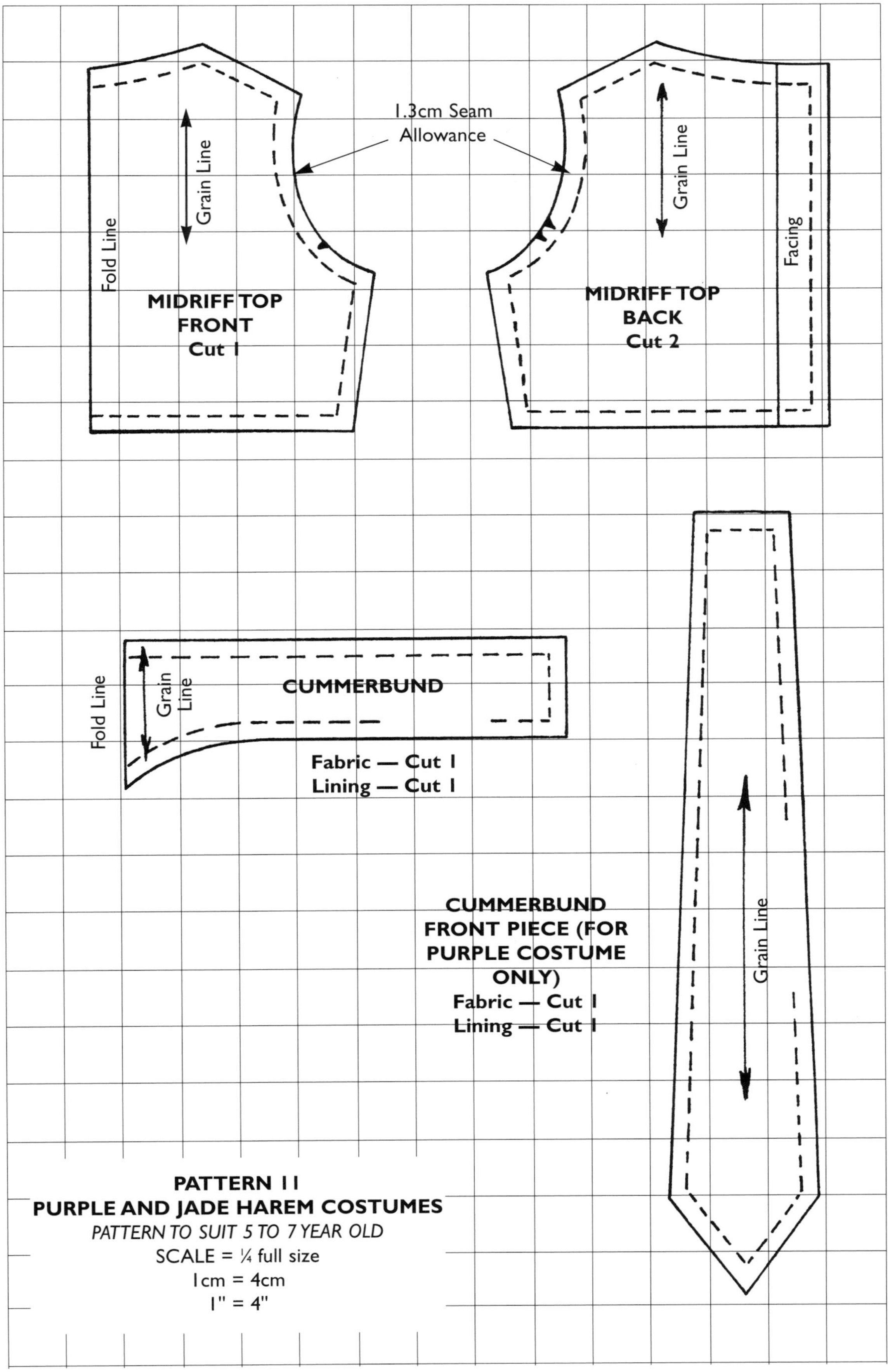

Grain Line

Fold Line

1.3cm Seam
Allowance

Grain Line

Facing

**MIDRIFF TOP
FRONT
Cut 1**

**MIDRIFF TOP
BACK
Cut 2**

Fold Line

Grain
Line

CUMMERBUND

**Fabric — Cut 1
Lining — Cut 1**

Grain Line

**CUMMERBUND
FRONT PIECE (FOR
PURPLE COSTUME
ONLY)
Fabric — Cut 1
Lining — Cut 1**

**PATTERN 11
PURPLE AND JADE HAREM COSTUMES**
PATTERN TO SUIT 5 TO 7 YEAR OLD
SCALE = ¼ full size
1cm = 4cm
1" = 4"

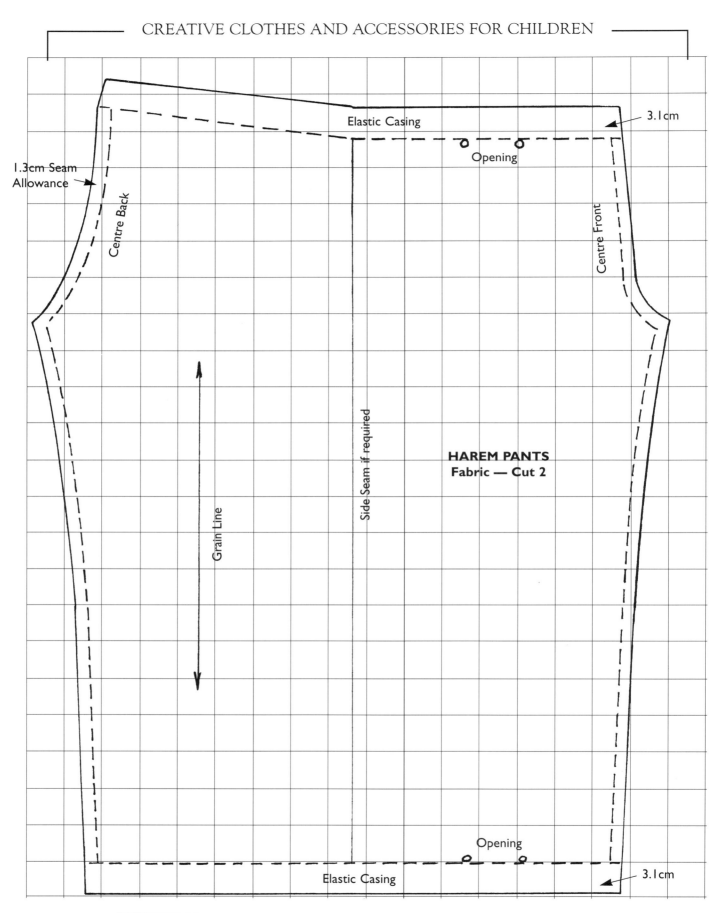

1.3cm Seam Allowance

Centre Back

Elastic Casing

3.1cm

Opening

Centre Front

Grain Line

Side Seam if required

HAREM PANTS
Fabric — Cut 2

Opening

Elastic Casing

3.1cm

PATTERN 11
PURPLE AND JADE HAREM COSTUMES (cont)
PATTERN TO SUIT 5 TO 7 YEAR OLD
SCALE = ¼ full size 1cm = 4cm 1" = 4"

12. CLOWN COSTUME

Children love dressing up as clowns and this happy costume is a delight to sew.

MATERIALS

 1.8m (2yd) green stretch material (for jacket and hat)

 1.25m (1⅜yd) of white stretch material (for trousers)

 1.8m (2yd) matching green taffeta (for jacket and hat lining)

 23cm (¼yd) striped material (for bib)

 70cm (¾yd) iron-on interfacing

 18cm (7in) white zip (for trousers)

 4 matching covered green buttons for jacket

 1 reel polyester white cotton

 1 reel matching polyester green cotton

 1 card of black fasteners

 30.5cm (12in) length of medium weight craft wire

 10cm (4in) square piece of red net.

METHOD

Jacket

1. Pin, tack and machine front to back at shoulders. (Fig 12.1) Press seams towards back. Repeat with lining.

2. Machine darts in back section. Repeat with lining. Cut through centre of darts almost to the point. Press flat open to allow darts to lie flat. Press up back facing towards the top. Overlock raw edges. (Fig 12.1)

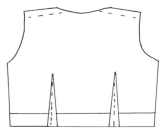

Fig 12.1 Machine front and back sections at shoulders. Repeat with lining. Machine darts and lining darts. Cut darts up in centre.

3. With right sides of front and back facing together, pin, tack and machine around neckline, down fronts and across bottom sections leaving side seams of jacket and lining open. (Fig 12.2) Trim seams and clip the whole area. Turn to right side and press flat.

Fig 12.2 Machine neck edge, fronts and back, bottom back and front curved sections.

4. With right sides of jacket and sleeves facing together, pin, tack and machine all around top of sleeves matching front and two back notches. Overlock seams and press towards the bottom. (Fig 12.3)

5. Pin and tack front and back together at side seams and machine in one continuous seam. Overlock seams and press towards the back. (Fig 12.3)

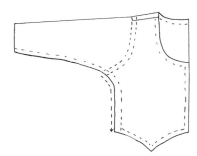

Fig 12.3 Machine sleeve into armhole. Machine front and back together at side seams in one continuous seam.

6. Fold up a 2.5cm (1in) seam on sleeve edges. Press flat and overlock edges.

7. Turn jacket to right side. Top stitch a 14mm (½in) seam all around edge of jacket and sleeves, ie. across the back, front, back neck and sleeve edges. (Fig 12.4)

Fig 12.4 Top-stitch all around edges of jacket and sleeves.

8. Press up a 14mm (½in) seam around edge of bib and machine. Hand-stitch press studs on bib and jacket where pattern indicates.

9. Machine buttonholes where pattern indicates. Hand-stitch buttons in centre of buttonholes. (Fig 12.5)

Fig 12.5 Sew and fasten bib in place. Machine buttonholes and stitch buttons in place.

Trousers

1. Pin, tack and machine darts on front and back sections. (Fig 12.6) Cut through centre of darts almost to the point. Press flat open to allow darts to lie flat.

2. With right sides facing together, pin and tack the two back sections together down centre back seam. Overlock edges. Press seam to one side. Repeat with front sections. (Fig 12.7)

3. With right sides facing together, machine front to back down inside legs. Overlock edges. (Fig 12.8)

4. Machine side seams of trousers. Press seams towards the back and overlock edges. (Fig 12.9)

5. Machine zip in place in back seam. *Refer to Setting in a Zip on page 100.*

Fig 12.6 Machine darts in front and back of trousers.

Fig 12.7 Machine two back sections together. Repeat with front.

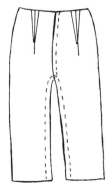

Fig 12.8 Machine front to back down inside leg.

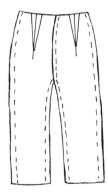

Fig 12.9 Machine side seams of trousers.

6. With right sides of straps facing together, fold over and machine.

7. Pin a safety pin to strap ends and pull to right side. Press flat.

8. Pin, tack and machine shoulder straps in place where indicated by circles on waistline, adjusting to a comfortable fit. (Fig 12.10)

9. Machine side seams of facings and press flat open. With right sides of trousers and facing together, pin, tack and machine facing to waistline matching side seams. (Fig 12.11) Turn facing to inside and press.

10. Overlock bottoms of trousers, press up a 2.5cm (1in) hem and hand-stitch. (Fig 12.12)

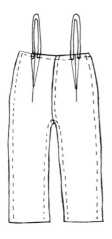

Fig 12.10 Machine the two straps then pin and machine straps to waistline.

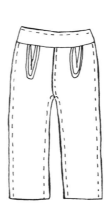

Fig 12.11 Machine facing to waistline.

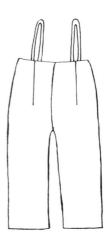

Fig 12.12 Press up hems on trousers, overlock edges and hand-stitch.

Clown Hat

1. Press iron-on interfacing to wrong side of hat crown. (Fig 12.13)

2. Press iron-on interfacing to middle section of hat. With right sides facing together, machine the back seam. Trim seam and press flat open. (Fig 12.14)

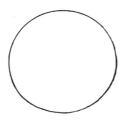

Fig 12.13 Press interfacing to wrong side of hat crown.

Fig 12.14 Press interfacing to middle section of hat. Machine back seam.

3. With right sides of hat crown and middle section facing each other, pin, tack and machine together. Clip all around seam and press seam towards bottom of hat. Repeat with lining sections (omitting interfacing). (Fig 12.15)

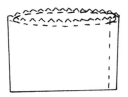

Fig 12.15 Machine crown to middle section. Clip seam.

4. With wrong sides of lining and hat facing together, drop lining into hat matching the two back seams. Baste together. (Lining and hat are now treated as one.)

5. Press interfacing to wrong side of one brim section. With right sides of the two brim sections facing each other, pin, tack and machine together. (Fig 12.16) Trim seam and clip all around edge. Turn hat brim to right side and press flat. Machine a top stitch 14mm (½in) from edge of brim all the way around. (Fig 12.17)

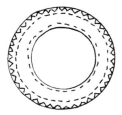

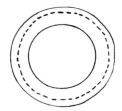

Fig 12.16 Press interfacing to one side of brim. Machine two brim sections together.

Fig 12.17 Turn brim to right side, press and top-stitch.

6. Pin and tack base of middle section to inside edge of brim, right sides facing together. Machine seam, clip and press flat. Fold remaining brim edge under 14mm (½in) then pin and hand-stitch to inside edge of brim. (Fig 12.18)

Fig 12.18 Machine base of middle section to inside edge of brim. Hand-slip down remaining edge.

7. To sew the net flower, cut out a circle of net 10cm (4in) in diameter. Fold circle in half then quarters to form a flute shape and hand-stitch together. Bend top of wire to form a loop and stitch to the net. (Fig 12.19) Make another loop at base of wire and hand-stitch to top of back seam of hat. (Fig 12.20)

Fig 12.19 Stitch net flower to top hook.

Fig 12.20 Stitch net flower to back seam of hat at the top.

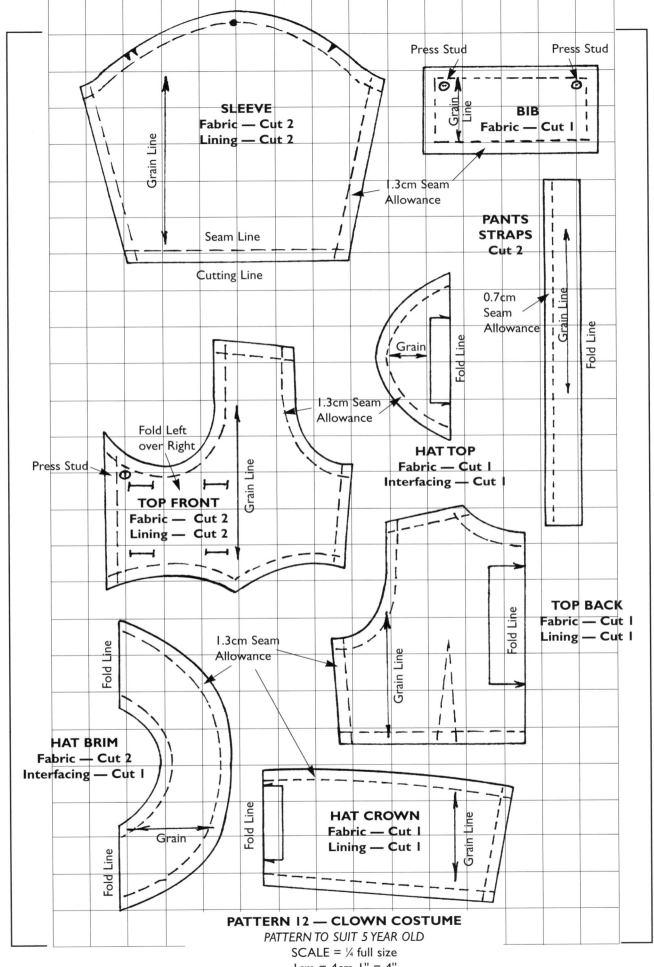

SLEEVE
Fabric — Cut 2
Lining — Cut 2

Grain Line

Seam Line

Cutting Line

Press Stud   Press Stud

Grain Line

BIB
Fabric — Cut 1

1.3cm Seam Allowance

PANTS STRAPS
Cut 2

0.7cm Seam Allowance

Grain Line

Fold Line

1.3cm Seam Allowance

Grain

Fold Line

HAT TOP
Fabric — Cut 1
Interfacing — Cut 1

Fold Left over Right

Press Stud

Grain Line

TOP FRONT
Fabric — Cut 2
Lining — Cut 2

Fold Line

TOP BACK
Fabric — Cut 1
Lining — Cut 1

Grain Line

1.3cm Seam Allowance

HAT BRIM
Fabric — Cut 2
Interfacing — Cut 1

Fold Line

Grain

Fold Line

Fold Line

HAT CROWN
Fabric — Cut 1
Lining — Cut 1

Grain Line

PATTERN 12 — CLOWN COSTUME
PATTERN TO SUIT 5 YEAR OLD
SCALE = ¼ full size
1cm = 4cm 1" = 4"

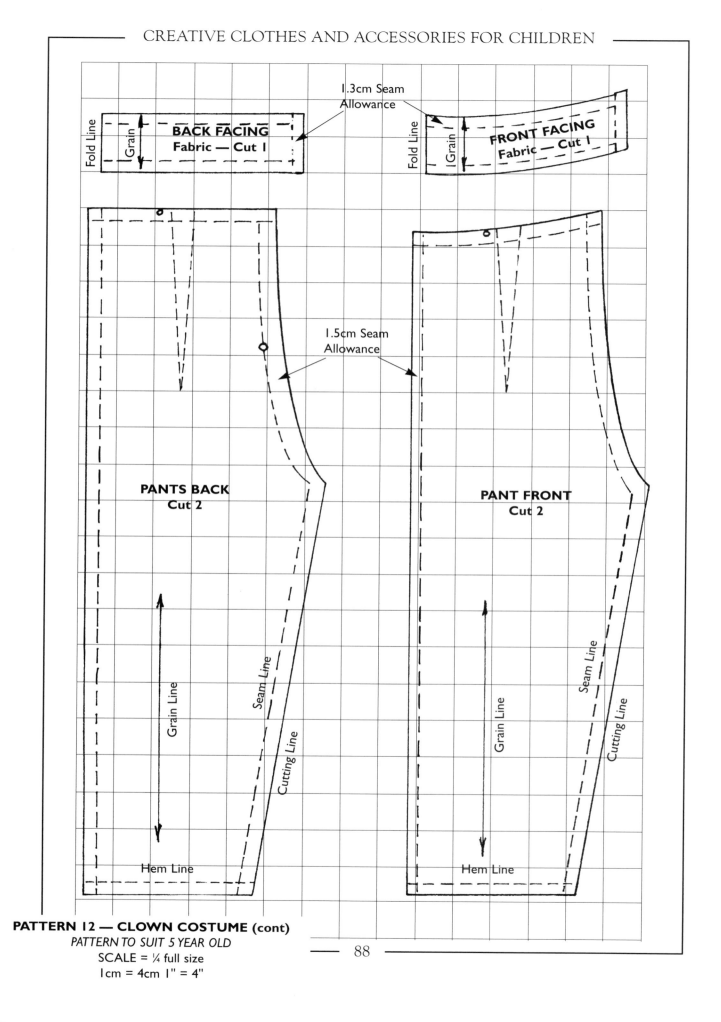

1.3cm Seam Allowance

BACK FACING
Fabric — Cut 1

Fold Line

Grain

FRONT FACING
Fabric — Cut 1

Fold Line

Grain

1.5cm Seam Allowance

PANTS BACK
Cut 2

Grain Line

Seam Line

Cutting Line

Hem Line

PANT FRONT
Cut 2

Grain Line

Seam Line

Cutting Line

Hem Line

PATTERN 12 — CLOWN COSTUME (cont)
PATTERN TO SUIT 5 YEAR OLD
SCALE = ¼ full size
1cm = 4cm 1" = 4"

Collars

13. BLACK VELVET AND LACE COLLAR

Detachable collars teamed with a basic frock or matching jumper can add a touch of chic to children's clothing as well as being very practical and easily laundered separately.

MATERIALS

    50cm (20in) of 90cm (36in) wide black velvet
    2m (2¼yd) of 2.5cm (1in) wide antique lace edging
    1 reel black polyester thread
    3 black fasteners
    50cm (20in) black taffeta for lining

METHOD
1. With right sides facing each other, pin collar and collar back sections together at shoulders. Repeat with lining.
2. With right sides of collar and lining facing together, pin back edge and opening of collar, continuing around the neck edge. Tack and machine.
3. Clip around neck edge of seam. Turn collar to right side and press flat. Fold and press a 2cm (¾in) seam over remaining raw edges of collar. Pin and hand-slip edges of collar and lining together.
4. On right side of collar, pin lace close to the edge, mitre corners and tack in place.
5. Hand-stitch edge of each side of the collar.
6. Fold back opening of collar, right side over left. Stitch three fasteners evenly placed on fold edge.

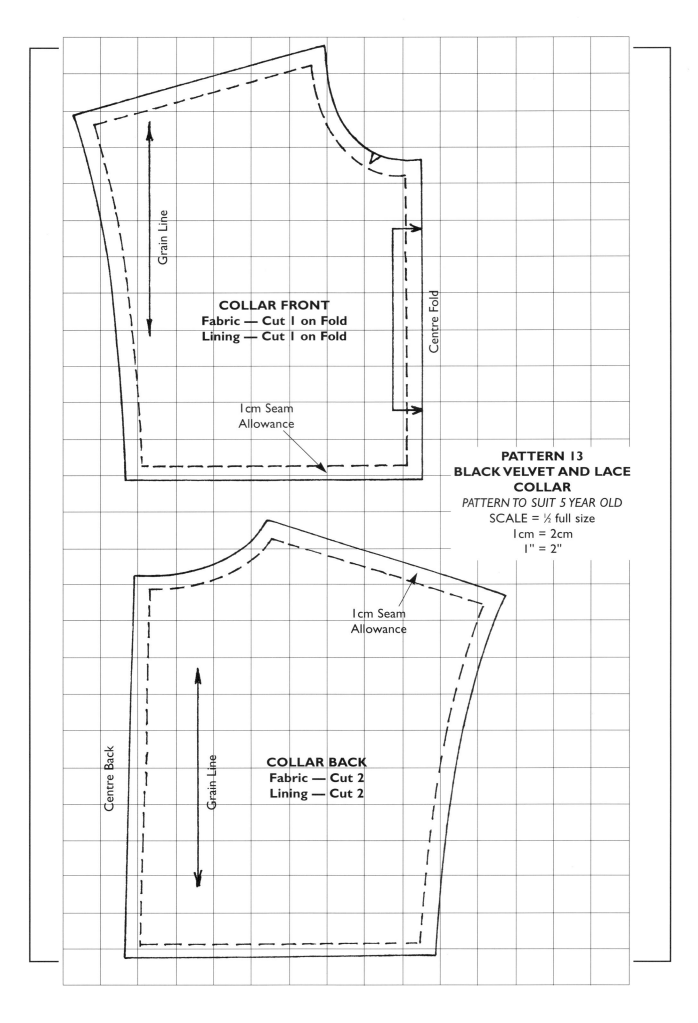

COLLAR FRONT
Fabric — Cut 1 on Fold
Lining — Cut 1 on Fold

Grain Line

Centre Fold

1cm Seam
Allowance

PATTERN 13
BLACK VELVET AND LACE
COLLAR
PATTERN TO SUIT 5 YEAR OLD
SCALE = ½ full size
1cm = 2cm
1" = 2"

1cm Seam
Allowance

Centre Back

Grain Line

COLLAR BACK
Fabric — Cut 2
Lining — Cut 2

14. CREAM LACE COLLAR

This collar is made from cream French lace and beaded with tiny cream pearls. It would look stunning on a black velvet or silk frock.

MATERIALS

45cm (½yd) of cream French lace

45cm (1/2yd) matching cream taffeta

1 reel matching polyester thread

1 packet cream seed pearls

1 pearl button

METHOD

1. After cutting out lace collar, bead the flowers to your own design.

2. To make pleated frill edge, measure collar circumference and cut a strip of the cream tafetta 2½ times the circumference length and 5cm (2in) wide. Join seams. Fold strip in half, wrong sides facing together, and fold over 14mm (½in) pleats all along.

3. With right sides of collar and pleating facing together, pin, tack and machine pleats on collar edge.

4. Machine a rouleau long enough to hold the pearl button in place. *Refer to Button Loops on page 105.* Tack loop to seam edge on right-hand side of back neck.

5. With right sides of collar and lining facing together, pin, tack and machine to circle openings. Turn collar to right side and press flat.

6. Hand-stitch pearl button in centre of loop.

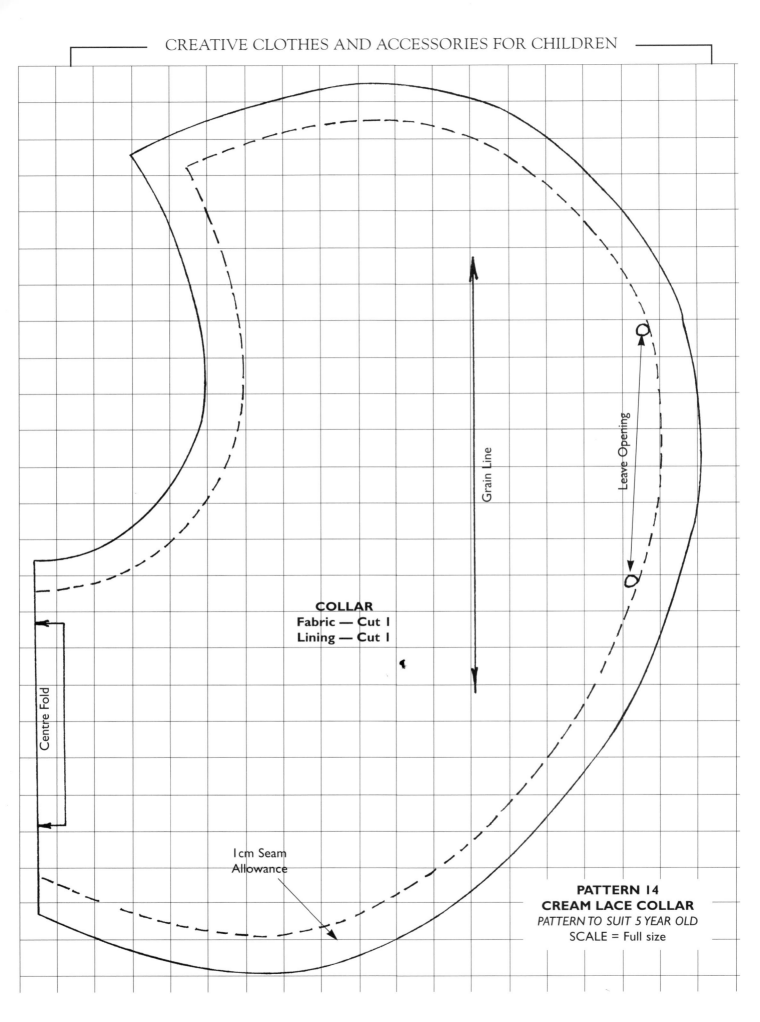

Grain Line

Leave Opening

COLLAR
Fabric — Cut 1
Lining — Cut 1

Centre Fold

1cm Seam
Allowance

PATTERN 14
CREAM LACE COLLAR
PATTERN TO SUIT 5 YEAR OLD
SCALE = Full size

Accessories

15. Dilly Bags

Dilly bags are fun to carry all sorts of special bits and pieces. A pretty frock with a matching bag is not only practical but makes a lovely accessory. You can sew them in all sizes — large ones for overnight stays with friends, huge ones to take to the library.

MATERIALS

    50cm (20in) of material (for bag)

    50cm (20in) matching taffeta (for lining)

    1 reel matching thread

    1.8m (2yd) matching cord

    4 beads (with large hole in centre)

    1 small matching tassel

    Small bunch of artificial flowers or handmade cloth
      roses (for trimming)

METHOD

1. With right sides of bag and lining facing together, machine across top seam line. (Fig 15.1) Repeat with other two sections. Press seams flat open.

2. Stitch roses in a group in centre of bag.

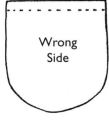

Wrong Side

Fig 15.1 Machine across top seam line.

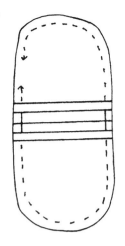

Fig 15.2 Machine all around the edge leaving a 5cm (2in) opening.

3. With right sides of bag and lining facing together and 2.5cm (1in) down on each side of centre seam, machine around the edge leaving a 5cm (2in) side opening unstitched. (Fig 15.2) Trim seam.

4. Turn bag to right side through side opening. Press flat with a warm iron.

5. Machine a row of stitching across and below drawstring openings all the way around on right side of bag. (Fig 15.3)

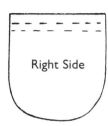

Right Side

Fig 15.3 Machine a row of stitching across and below drawstring openings.

6. Pin a safety pin to cord ends and thread through from one end of the opening to the other. (Fig 15.4) Cut cords, leaving 25cm (10in) long ties. Repeat cord threading at opposite end of opening.

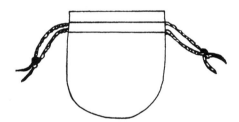

Fig 15.4 Thread cord through drawstring openings.

7. Thread each end of the four cords through a bead. Tie a knot to hold beads in place. Hand-stitch tassel in place at centre bottom of bag. (Fig 15.5)

Fig 15.5 Thread beads through cord ends. Stitch flowers in centre of bag. Hand-stitch tassel in place.

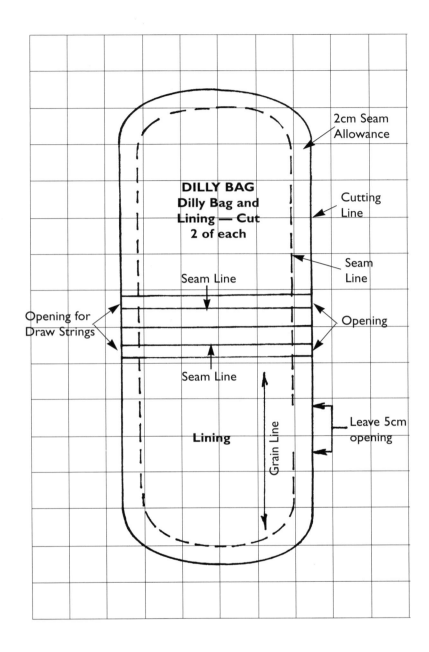

PATTERN 15
DILLY BAG
SCALE = ¼ full size
1cm = 4cm
1" = 4"

16. CLOTH ROSES

Cloth roses are so easy to make and can add a very glamorous finish to garments and accessories. Depending on how elaborate you want the finished garment to look, stamens or drop pearls can be assembled in the centres of roses to add an extra touch to bridal or evening wear.

HANDY TIPS

- Make a sample rose the size you need then unpick it and use as a pattern.
- Material must always be cut on the bias.
- Do not use material that is too heavy or thick or the roses will be too bulky.
- Save left-over materials and you will be able to make many different coloured cloth roses.

MATERIALS

Material of your choice

Matching thread

Fine sewing needle

Drop pearls or stamens (optional)

METHOD

1. Make a paper pattern the size you need for the rose. Cut out pattern on bias of material. (Fig 16.1)

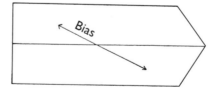

Fig 16.1 Cut out rose from pattern on bias of material.

2. Fold material in half lengthwise, wrong sides together. Machine a gathering stitch 6mm (¼in) from raw edge. (Fig 16.2)

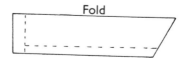

Fig 16.2 Fold material in half with wrong sides facing together. Machine a gathering stitch 6mm (¼in) from edge.

3. To form centre of rose, fold pointed end three times into a pyramid shape and stitch securely. Repeat another three times. (Fig 16.3)

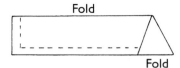

Fig 16.3 Fold pointed end three times in a pyramid shape.

4. Start pulling up gathering stitch and hand-stitch in place at sections. (Fig 16.4)

Fig 16.4 Pull up gathering stitch and stitch in place.

5. Tuck in raw edge 14mm (½in) at the end and stitch at base. Cut bulk away from base. (Fig 16.5)

Fig 16.5 Tuck in raw end and stitch. Cut bulk away from base.

6. To use roses in a bouquet, cut wire the required length and make a stem.

7. Bend a little hook with long nose pliers and stitch hook to base of rose using a needle and double thread. Wind a length of florist tape over the hook and base. Secure with a dab of glue.

17. GIRL'S SNOOD

MATERIALS
   1 ball 4ply cotton
   3mm (⅛in) crochet hook

METHOD
Make 6ch, join with a slip to form a ring.

Round 1: 3ch, 23tr in ring, sl st in 3rd ch at beg (24tr counting 3ch as tr).

Round 2: 3ch, 1tr in same place as sl st, 2tr in each tr to end, sl st in 3rd ch at beg (48tr).

Round 3: 3ch, 1tr in same place as sl st, 3ch, miss 1tr, 1dc in next tr, 3ch, miss 1tr, * 2tr in next tr, 3ch, miss 1tr, 1dc in next tr, 3ch, miss 1tr, rep from * to end, sl st in 3rd ch at beg (12 patts).

Round 4: 3ch, 1tr in next tr, 2ch, 1dc in next loop, 5ch, 1dc in next loop, 2ch * 1tr in each of next 2tr, 2ch, 1dc in next loop, 5ch, 1dc in next loop, 2ch, rep from * to end, sl st in 3rd ch at beg.

Round 5: 3 ch, 1tr in next tr, 4ch, 1dc in 5ch loop, 4ch * 1tr in each of next 2tr, 4ch, 1dc in 5ch loop, 4ch rep from * to end, sl st in 3rd ch at beg.

Rep 4th and 5th rounds 7 times (14 rows) or until required length. This length can be worn at the nape of the neck. To wear the snood from the top of the head, add more rows to fit.

Next Round: 3ch, 1tr in next tr * 3ch, 1 long tr in dc, 3ch, 1tr in each of next 2tr, rep from * ending with sl st in 3rd ch at beg.

Next Round: 1dc in each ch to end, sl st in 1st dc.

Next Round: 1dc in 1st st * 3ch miss 1dc, 1dc in next dc. Rep from * ending with 3ch sl st in 1st dc. Pull thread through and neaten off.

Thread hat elastic or fine ribbon through the holes. The snood can then be worn at the nape of the neck or, in the longer version, from the top of the head perhaps attached to a headband.

ABBREVIATIONS

beg	Beginning
ch	Chain
dc	Double crochet
dec	Decrease
patt	Pattern
rep	Repeat
sl st	Slip stitch
tr	Treble

Sewing Techniques

A. SETTING IN A ZIP

The lapped application method is used in skirts and frocks. Side zips are sewn in on the left, so the lap section is facing towards the back and you cannot look directly at the teeth. Use the zipper foot attachment on your machine to help you sew close to the zip edge. Test the zip before you use it by pulling it up and down to make sure it runs freely. Remember, you must always tack a zip in place and the teeth should never be visible when wearing your garment.

THREE POINTS TO REMEMBER

- Tack a zip in place
- Use a zipper foot
- Pull the head of the zip down out of the way until you pass that sewing area

Fig A1. Zip seam area

METHOD

1. Follow your pattern's instructions on how your zip seam area should be completed before setting in your zip. (Fig A1)
2. Pull your zip up and down to test it is not faulty.
3. With the right side of the garment facing you, fold over each side of the top of the zip. Hand-stitch in place.
4. Still with the right side of the garment facing you, pin the closed zip from top to bottom next to the fold on the right-hand side. On the other side (which now becomes the lap side) pin the zip 6mm (¼in) from the fold line from bottom to top.

5. Tack the zip in place to prevent it from moving, sewing bigger tacking stitches at the back (they are easier to remove). Use the same colour thread as your garment. The little tacking stitches, which are now visible on the right side will help as a guide to sew straight. (Fig A2)

6. Put zipper foot in position on your machine. Check that there is enough thread in the bobbin to complete the sewing of this section of the zip in one step.

7. Start machining from the top of the lap side. First, pull the zip down 2cm (¾in) and sew this section. Lift the pressure foot, pull the zipper head back up and lower the foot, and then continue sewing down to the bottom of the zip. (Fig A3)

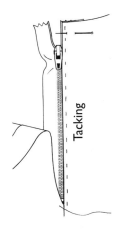

Fig A2. Pin zipper next to fold.

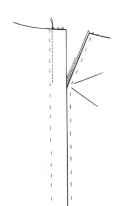

Fig A3. Start machining from top of lap side. Pull down head of zipper.

8. Pivot the fabric to sew across the bottom of the zip. Pivot again before going up the other side.

9. Continue sewing up towards the top. Stop 2cm (¾in) away from the top and pull the zipper head down and out of the way before sewing up to the top.

10. Remove tacking from the back, cutting threads out. (Fig A4)

11. Stitch a hook at the top of the zip on the flap side, a little back from the edge. Sewing with a double thread and a knot, again a little back from the edge, make a double loop the size of the hook and blanket-stitch along its length. The hook and eye should not be visible when the person is wearing the garment.

12. Place a cloth over the zip and press lightly.

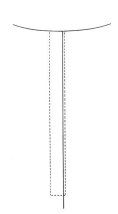

Fig A4. Finished zipper, no teeth visible.

B. SLEEVES

Set-in Sleeve

A set-in sleeve is a very tailored sleeve moulded into the armhole with no gathers. The sleeve pattern will have one notch at the front of the sleeve and two notches at the back. The back of the sleeve has extra measurement to allow for the movement of the body.

METHOD

1. Using the largest stitch on your machine, sew a gathering row on the seam line at the top of the sleeve, starting at the front notch and going around to the two back notches. (Fig B1)

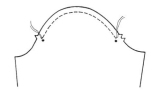

Fig B1 Gathering stitch between notches

2. Stitch the underarm seam, neaten and press flat open. (Fig B2)

Fig B2 Stitching underseam

3. Turn the sleeve to the right side.
4. Hold the garment so you are looking into the armhole. Drop the sleeve into the armhole, right sides facing each other.
5. Match the seam lines and notches together. Pin top of sleeve to the shoulder seam, underarm seam to underarm seam, notches to notches. The area between the notches is where you ease in the sleeve. Because the sleeve is slightly larger than the armhole at this stage, use the gathering thread to slightly ease the material to fit neatly into the armhole. The gathering thread is

only to mould the sleeve head in place. There should be no puckering. (Fig B3)

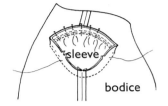

Fig B3 Pin and tack sleeve in place

6. Tack in place all around the armhole.

7. Machine a little below the tacking, then remove the tacking, being careful not to stretch the armhole.

8. Sew a second row of stitching 6mm (¼in) away from sewing line, within the seam allowance.

9. Trim any bulk away. (Fig B4)

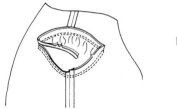

Fig B4

10. Press armhole seam (holding shoulder pad underneath) down towards the bottom of sleeve.

C. ROULEAUS

Rouleaus are ties or cylindrical strips of fabric. They are made from strips of material cut on the bias, which after machining are pulled through themselves to form ties. They are used for shoulder straps, and are traditionally used for the loops that fasten covered buttons on the backs of wedding and evening gowns in place of zip openings. Hand-stitched into daisy flower shapes and beaded with tiny seed beads they give millinery, gowns and crafts a fashionable finish.

METHOD

1. To make shoulder straps, measure the length required for the strap plus a seam allowance.
2. Cut bias strips 2.5cm (1in) wide and the length required.
3. Fold the strip in half, right sides together, so that the edges are even.
4. Stitch a 6mm (¼in) seam along its length.
5. Thread a darning needle with fancywork cotton. For strength, make a small knot at the end.
6. Sew thread through end of strip to fasten. (Fig C1)

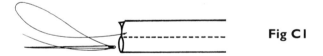

Fig C1

7. Insert the eye of the needle into the strip and slide it through to the other end. (Fig C2) Gently pull through to the end, cut off thread. Do not press rouleaus.

Fig C2

D. BUTTON LOOPS

Button loops are made from rouleaus in the same fabric as the garment. For additional information refer to Rouleaus on page 104.

METHOD
1. Cut bias strips, 2.5cm (1in) wide. The length will depend on the number of button loops required.
2. Fold the strip in half, right sides together, so that the edges are even.
3. Stitch a 6mm (¼in) seam along its length.
4. Thread a darning needle with fancywork cotton. For strength, make a small knot at the end and use to pull rouleau through itself to the right side.

Button Loop Closure

1. Always make a test loop to check that it is the right size to fit easily over the button. It must fit correctly to hold garment edges securely closed.
2. For back closures, loops are sewn in position on the left-hand side of the back and buttons on the right-hand side.
3. Place the centre of the button on the seam line, 6mm (¼in) from the edge and lay tubing around it with seam side up. With a needle and double thread, fasten the loop at the top and bottom. Cut the loop.
4. Complete the finished edges of the garment according to your pattern instructions. Mark button placement positions, then sew buttons securely to the garment.

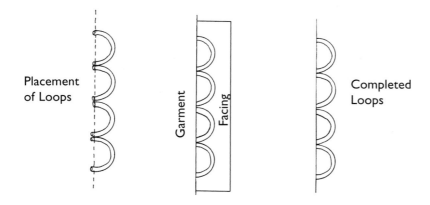

Placement of Loops

Garment Facing

Completed Loops

E. BINDINGS

Double Binding

Bindings are a neat and practical finish around necklines or sleeveless armholes. Made in a contrast colour they can give a very attractive finish. Make sure if you are using a colour contrast that the binding fabric is the same texture as the main fabric. This way the tension of the materials will be even and the bindings will lie flat. Check whether the fabric should be pre-washed to prevent shrinking later on.

METHOD

1. Measure the length of the area you are binding. Allow 2.5cm (1in) for seam allowance.

2. Cut bias strip 3.1cm (1⅛in) wide.

3. With wrong sides together, press binding in half.

4. When binding a neckline, make the join at the shoulder. Never make a join in the front or back of the neckline. Armhole bindings should join at the side seam under the arm.

5. Pin the binding on the right side of the garment. Tack and machine along seam line. Remove tacking. (Fig E1)

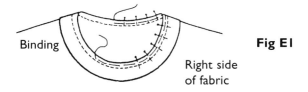

Binding   **Fig E1**

Right side of fabric

6. Trim seam allowance evenly and press the binding strip up towards the top. (Fig E2)

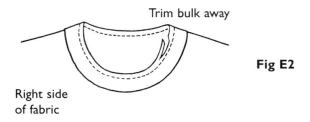

Trim bulk away

Fig E2

Right side of fabric

7. Flip the binding over the raw edge to the wrong side of the garment. This forms what is called a 'wall' and must stand upright. Slip-stitch a hem on the raw edge of the binding. (Fig E3)

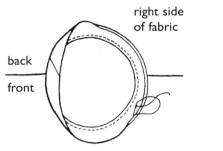

right side
of fabric

Fig E3

back

front

fold binding to the wrong side

8. On the right side of the garment, pin in the ditch, which means in the gutter of the seam directly below the wall. Tack in place with matching thread. Use bigger stitches at the back as they are easier to remove.

9. Change sewing machine foot to a zipper foot. This makes it easier to sew in the ditch and not on the binding. Remove tacking from back, cutting thread away. (Fig E4)

Fig E4

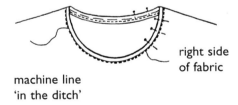

right side
of fabric

machine line
'in the ditch'

10. Hold a shoulder pad under the binding and press with a warm iron. (Fig E5)

Fig E5

finished binding

F. FLUTING EDGES

Fluting hems, frills or sleeve edges gives a soft flowing movement to a garment. When fluting silk, organza, satin or tulle, use a 15kg (30lb) weight fishing line, clear in colour. Allow 10cm (4in) extra to the length of the garments, etc. as the edges will spring up shorter once the fishing line starts fluting. Practice with a sample of material before sewing.

MATERIALS

    1 reel clear 15kg (30lb) weight fishing line
    Matching polyester thread

METHOD

1. Set machine stitching dial on the smallest zigzag stitch.
2. Turn stitch length to just below number one on the dial.
3. Turn tension dial to basic sewing.
4. Before commencing fluting, extend the fishing line 5cm (2in) beyond the material.
5. Fold over the edge of the material 6mm (¼in) to just cover the fishing line. The machine will sew a very close buttonhole stitch over the fishing line.
6. When edge is completed, cut off excess line and join ends with a hand-sewn buttonhole stitch.